From Prophecy to Reality

Approaching Week 70

WALT THRUN

WESTBOW
PRESS®
A DIVISION OF THOMAS NELSON
& ZONDERVAN

WestBow Press books may be ordered through booksellers or by contacting:

WestBow Press
A Division of Thomas Nelson & Zondervan
1663 Liberty Drive
Bloomington, IN 47403
www.westbowpress.com
1 (866) 928-1240

ISBN: 978-1-9736-3440-9 (sc)
ISBN: 978-1-9736-3441-6 (e)

Print information available on the last page.

WestBow Press rev. date: 08/14/2018

Contents

After the initial sin in the Garden, Adam and Eve attempted to cover their sin and hide from the presence of God. They were banished from the Garden; however, God had provided them a new covering of animal skins. This was the initial step by God to bring them back to His presence.

The presence of God will be followed from the Garden, through the tabernacle, through the temples, through the presence of the Holy Spirit within believers during the church age, through the Millennial Temple, and culminating in the descent of eternal New Jerusalem.

Return and repent are the first steps required to be once again in God's presence. Both words carry the meaning of 'again,' or 'to go back.' And both words likewise require a proactive God to inspire repentance in a man's heart.

Interestingly, the word 'progress' is not found in either the Hebrew or Greek Biblical dictionaries. However, 'progressivism' is a very popular political ideology in America today.

Redemption is also initiated by God. Redemption means basically to buy something back that was lost. That which was lost included the extensive consequences of the curse, plus life itself.

There are three components of redemption, i.e. a lost possession, a redemptive price and a close relative willing to pay the required price. Only the redeemed will be in the eternal presence of God.

Abraham's 'Seed' is as relevant today as it was two millennia ago. During the church age, those who are of faith are sons of Abraham. This chapter will also discuss the differences between Abraham's physical seeds and his spiritual seeds. The ongoing battle is between Abraham's son born according to the flesh and his son born according to God's promise.

The benchmark for 'truth' is the word of God, inasmuch as it is impossible for God to lie.

The distortion of truth begins with deception, while deception begins with a lie. Such preceded man's first sin in the Garden of Eden.

After the fall, man's heart has been innately deceitful from birth.

Straying from Biblical truth also causes division and apostasy. Such paves the way for many anti-Christs.

Idolatry has been a major factor in the history of all nations, including Israel.

As history progressed, idolatry thrived. However, while idols of today have become more subtle, they are equally devastating.

The premise is suggested that the most prevalent and destructive idol of today is the love of mammon.

There is no glory when suffering the consequences of one's own actions; however, there is glory for suffering for Christ's sake, as well as future rewards for the sufferer.

Suffering can be physical, emotional, or in the form of persecution. To be able to suffer in any way for Christ is a gift of the Holy Spirit.

All Christians will suffer.

Persecution of saints will be avenged by God Himself in His timing.

Tyre is the most detailed example of a nation's misdirected priorities in the Bible.

Tyre is all about mercantilism and man's insatiable appetite for that which is desired, but not necessary.

This chapter presents the challenges to determine if America and her priorities match those of Tyre and her merchants.

The future fall of Tyre is explained in detail in Revelation Chapter 18.

Like Tyre, Babylon also has both near-term and long-term implications.

Babylon fell to the Medes and Persians in the sixth century BC, but that which Babylon represented will reappear by the end of the age, and mighty Babylon will be without remedy.

A question similar to that of Tyre is whether or not America has adopted Babylonian characteristics, and if so what will be the consequences?

The eternal fall of Babylon is also detailed in Revelation chapter 18.

A major emphasis of this chapter is geographic, especially the Fertile Crescent, and specifically the land of Shinar.

A significant prophecy is examined where Zechariah observes an ephah containing a woman described as evil being transported to 'its base' in the land of Shinar. The ephah with its lead cover represents secularism and materialism.

At the end of the chapter several questions are posed to allow one to determine if there are similarities between several present representative Middle Eastern nations, and the feet and toes of Nebuchadnezzar's metallic image of predominant kingdoms of his era.

Inasmuch as two succeeding chapters focus on the timing of significant future events, it seemed beneficial to present a brief synopsis of 'time' as presented in the Scriptures.

Increments of time in the Bible range from specific hours to millenniums.

Both the beginning and end of time are addressed.

The day of the Lord refers to the approaching return of Jesus Christ to reclaim all that He paid for at Calvary.

It is a time never before equaled in history where the required wrath of God is released on unrepentant mankind.

The day of the Lord will usher in the millennial kingdom.

The title words describe that which God will do following the great tribulation in preparation for Christ's thousand year reign from Jerusalem.

Again, the title words are proactive steps initiated by God.

This chapter describes characteristics of the approaching earthly millennial kingdom.

Prophetically, the focus is the fulfillment of God's numerous promises made to Abraham and his descendents.

But the end is not yet.

The word 'remember' is similar to the other 're' words previously discussed.

'Remember' basically means to 'bring to mind again.'

In the Old Testament God's people were told to remember His mighty works which He had done on their behalf. His people were also told to remember His laws and commandments.

In the New Testament God's people were told to remember the words of Jesus. A major part of the Holy Spirit's ministry was to remind God's people of all that Jesus had said and done.

However, the final thought is what God would not remember.

Introduction to

From Prophecy to Reality:
Approaching Week 70

There are two major objectives of this book. The first is to review God's plan to bring fallen man back to His presence, as it was in the beginning.

The initial seven chapters will focus on this objective by examining God's initiatives, plus obstacles and conditions prevalent during the current church age.

Several key words found in these chapters include 'return,' 'repent,' 'redeem,' 'renew,' and 'restore.' Such 're' words basically mean to go back again to where man, or a nation, was before separation from God.

Solomon summed up the premise wonderfully and succinctly.

"That which has been is what will be, that which is done is what will be done, and there is nothing new under the

sun. Is there anything of which it may be said, 'See, this is new'? It has already been in ancient times before us." Ecclesiastes 1:9-10 NKJV

The future of the nations

The second objective builds on the first, i.e. to consider the future of the nations, particularly America.

Prophecy typically has both short-term as well as long-term implications. For example, both Tyre and Babylon fell in history because of their disregard of God and their mistreatment of Israel. In the future, the characteristics of both Tyre and Babylon will reappear in the nations to be judged in the 'Day of the LORD.'

The apostle John records the reasons for the judgment of the nations upon Christ's return.

"For all the nations have drunk of the wine of the wrath of her (the mother of harlots) fornication, the kings of the earth have committed fornication with her, and the merchants of the earth have become rich through the abundance of her luxury." Revelation 18:3 NKJV

The role of Israel's history in the future of the nations

The Bible provides much insight into America's future based on Israel's past. God revealed His standard of righteousness to Israel for all nations to observe - and emulate.

The Book of Deuteronomy, which was written during the final month of Israel's 40 year post Exodus journey, summarized Israel's history up to that point; particularly the events and instructions given during those 40 years. God's revelations to Israel during that time period serve as the benchmark for all nations from that point on.

An extremely significant Scripture, written 1,500 years after Deuteronomy, confirms the timelessness of the lessons learned during that time period.

"Now all these things (summarized in Deuteronomy) happened to them (Israel) as examples, and they were written for our admonition (instruction), upon whom the ends of the ages have come." 1 Corinthians 10:11 NKJV

The history of other nations will also shed much light on America's future.

Present and future events and ideologies are being patterned after past history. Simply stated, history is repeating itself.

Questions will be frequently posed, relative to America's laws and priorities, to allow the reader to determine if such laws and priorities are consistent with actions deserving God's judgment.

The sequence of the chapters of this book attempts to chronologically present the journey from Christ's ascension to His return to establish the millennial kingdom.

To aid in understanding, the Table of Contents will include a brief synopsis of each chapter's content, allowing the reader to choose his/her order of study.

Chapter 1

Man in the Presence of God

The ultimate bliss for man is to be in the presence of the One who created him. The story begins in the Garden of Eden when man was created in the very image of God.

And the LORD God formed man of the dust of the ground, and breathed into his nostrils the breath of life; and man became a living soul. Genesis 2:7 KJV

'Breath' is synonymous with 'spirit.'

In the garden Adam and Eve lived in the very presence of God.

There were two significant trees in the garden: the tree of life and the tree of the knowledge of good and evil.

While Adam and Eve had access to the tree of life, they were denied access to the tree of knowledge of good and evil. Thus the devil tempted Eve to partake of the tree of which they were denied.

Eve did, in fact, succumb to the devil's cunning deception. Having partaken of the tree of knowledge of good and evil, their eyes were opened and Eve and her husband became aware of their sin of disobedience.

And they heard the voice of the LORD God walking in the garden in the cool of the day: and Adam and his wife hid themselves from the presence of the LORD God... Genesis 3:8 KJV

Their guilt caused them to attempt to hide from the presence of their Creator.

This is a major point; man attempted to hide from God. However, God in His mercy would be proactive, from that time forward, in bringing man back into His presence.

Redemption begins

God sent Adam and Eve out of the garden so they could not partake of the tree of life in their sinful position.

Recall, however, that God had clothed them in the skins of animals to replace their covering of fig leaves.

Since Adam and Eve, all mankind has been born without the spirit of God.

A major step taken by God to renew His presence among men

To focus on the point of man being in the presence of God, let's fast forward to the time shortly after God delivered the fledgling nation of Israel from Egyptian bondage. God's servant during that time was Moses who was appointed to be God's spokesman both to the Israelites and to Pharaoh.

After the incredible Exodus, God gave Moses instructions for building a place where God could be present with His people. The place would be called a 'sanctuary' which would be patterned after the heavenly.

And the glory of the LORD rested on Mount Sinai...Then the LORD spoke to Moses, saying, "Tell the sons of Israel to raise a contribution for Me...and let them construct a sanctuary for Me, that I may dwell among them."
Exodus 24:16, 25:1-2, 8 NASB

God told Moses that He wanted to dwell among His people. The sanctuary would also include specific furnishings to represent the way to approach the Holy God.

According to all that I show thee, after the pattern of the tabernacle, and the pattern of all the furnishings thereof, even so shall ye make it. Exodus 25:9 KJV

The 'tabernacle' has a more specific meaning than 'sanctuary.' Tabernacle means 'residence,' 'dwelling place,' and 'presence of God.' The tabernacle would be within the sanctuary.

God stressed to Moses that the sanctuary and tabernacle must be built exactly to God's instructions per the master pattern.

And so it was; the components were completed and the tabernacle was erected on the first day, of the first month, of the second year after the Exodus. This would place the timing fifteen days less than a year after the initial Passover, or 1444 BC.

The outer court of the sanctuary measured 150 ft x 75 ft while the tabernacle itself measured 45 ft x 15 ft x 15 ft.

The tabernacle was further divided into the holy place and the most holy place. The holy place where the lampstand, table of showbread, and incense altar were located measured 30 ft x 15 ft while the most holy place where the ark and mercy seat were located was a cube measuring 15 ft x 15 ft x 15 ft.

Then a cloud covered the tent of the congregation, and the glory of the LORD filled the tabernacle.
Exodus 40:34 KJV

God would reside within the tabernacle throughout the wilderness journey years.

The journey of the ark of the tabernacle

Recall, the tabernacle and its furnishings were completed in the beginning of the second year after the Exodus and would be the place where God would talk with Moses and give instructions during the remaining years of the wilderness journey.

And there I will meet with thee, and I will commune with thee from above the mercy seat, from between the two cherubim which are upon the ark of the testimony, of all things which I will give thee in commandment unto the children of Israel. Exodus 25:22 KJV

Consider the first verse in the Book of Leviticus.

And the LORD called unto Moses, and spoke unto him out of the tabernacle of the congregation... Leviticus 1:1 KJV

The Book of Numbers begins with the same statement.

The Ark of the Covenant was considered to represent the very presence of God. However, there were times when the ark was removed from the tabernacle to represent God's presence during significant events.

Recall the explicit instructions when crossing the River Jordan and the subsequent taking the city of Jericho. Both of those major events included the priests carrying the ark outside the tabernacle.

The tabernacle was subsequently set up in the town of Shiloh located approximately 30 miles north of Jerusalem.

And the whole congregation of the children of Israel assembled together at Shiloh, and set up the tabernacle of the congregation there. And the land was subdued before them. Joshua 18:1 KJV

The tabernacle and Ark of the Covenant were prevalent throughout the time of the Judges.

Misusing and abusing the Ark of the Covenant

Now when the LORD directed the ark to be carried, all was fine; but when the people used the ark as a symbol of God's presence and power without His direction, things didn't go so well.

Israel's enemies, as well as Israel herself, learned that lesson the hard way.

During a battle with the Philistines, shortly after young Samuel was established as a prophet in Shiloh, Israel was defeated and 4,000 of their men of war were killed. Israel didn't understand the defeat. Their solution:

Let us fetch the ark of the covenant of the LORD out of Shiloh unto us, that, when it cometh among us, it may save us out of the hand of our enemies. 1 Samuel 4:3b KJV

When the ark arrived the Israelites shouted so loud with joy that it stirred the Philistines. Then the Philistines learned that the reason for the joy was the arrival of the ark into the war zone.

Woe unto us! Who shall deliver us out of the hand of these mighty gods? These are the gods that smote the Egyptians with all the plagues in the wilderness. 1 Samuel 4:8 KJV

Nevertheless, the Philistines fought with great vigor and again won the next battle, this time killing 30,000 Israeli men of war including the two sons of Eli, and capturing the ark of God.

God left the tabernacle

The stress of losing that battle caused the death of the aged Eli. The wife of Phinehas, one of Eli's sons killed in that battle, shortly thereafter died during child birth, but not before naming her newborn son Ichabod, meaning 'the glory has departed from Israel.'

The Psalmist subsequently confirmed that God had forsaken His tabernacle.

...So that he forsook the tabernacle of Shiloh, the tent which he placed among men, and delivered his strength into captivity... Psalm 78:60-61 KJV

The ark in the hands of the enemy

The misfortunes experienced by the Philistines after capturing the ark are humorous.

The Philistines took the ark and placed it in the temple of their pagan god Dagon. Their naïve thinking was that such placement would supposedly show the superiority of Dagon over the God of the Hebrews.

However, on the very next day, the Philistines found Dagon fallen on his face before the ark of the LORD. So they set him up again in the presence of the ark.

But early on the next morning they found Dagon on his face again before the ark, but in addition:

...and the head of Dagon and both the palms of his hands were cut off upon the threshold; only the stump of Dagon was left to him. 1 Samuel 5:4b KJV

The Philistines then took major efforts to return the ark to the Israelites.

The ark back in the hands of the Jews

The Philistines have brought again the ark of the LORD; come ye down, and fetch it up to you...And the men of Kiriath-jearim came, and fetched up the ark of the LORD, and brought in into the house of Abinadab... 1 Samuel 6:21b-7:1 KJV

The ark remained in the house of Abinadab for 20 years until the rule of David.

And David again gathered all the chosen men of Israel...
to bring up...the ark of God...so they brought...the ark of
God from the house of Abinadab...and set it in its place
inside the tent which David had pitched for...
2 Samuel 6:1, 4, 17 NASB

It was after David was anointed King over all of Israel that he brought the Ark of the Covenant from the house of Abinadab to the tent that he had erected in Jerusalem.

The glory of the LORD had departed from the tabernacle while it was in Shiloh, since it became little more than a tangible symbol of God, rather than the very presence of God.

One day while David was enjoying his own great house he realized that the ark didn't have a house like his, but rather was kept in a tent behind curtains.

David told the prophet Nathan that it was time to build a grand house for the ark. Nathan agreed; however, God had different plans.

God told Nathan to tell David that he could not build a temple for the ark, but rather his son who was yet to be born would build the temple for the ark.

"When your days are complete and you lie down with your fathers, I will raise up your descendant after you, who will come forth from you and I will establish his kingdom. He shall build a house for My name, and I will establish the throne of his kingdom forever." 2 Samuel 7:12-13 NASB

After David's son by Bathsheba, born out of wedlock died, David took Bathsheba for his wife.

And David comforted Bathsheba, his wife, and went in unto her, and lay with her; and she bore a son, and he called his name Solomon; and the LORD loved him. 2 Samuel 12:24 KJV

From tent to temple

As David grew old he told his son Solomon what God had told him through Nathan the prophet.

And of all my sons (for the LORD hath given me many sons) he hath chosen Solomon, my son, to sit upon the throne of the kingdom of the LORD over Israel. And he said unto me, Solomon, thy son, shall build my house...for I have chosen him to be my son... 1 Chronicles 28:5-6 KJV

And so it was.

And it came to pass in the four hundred and eightieth year after the children of Israel were come out of the land of Egypt, in the fourth year of Solomon's reign over Israel...that he began to build the house of the LORD. 1 Kings 6:1 KJV

The building of Solomon's temple

Therefore, construction of Solomon's temple began in 965 BC. The house (temple) took seven years to build.

The holy place measured 60 ft x 30 ft x 45 ft high, but the most holy place measured 30 ft x 30 ft x 30 ft. The dimensions of the most holy place in Solomon's temple were exactly twice those of the most holy place in the tabernacle. However, 15 ft cubed is just 3,375 cubic feet while 30 ft cubed is 27,000 cubic feet. Therefore the volume of the most holy place of Solomon's temple was 8 times larger than that of the most holy place of the tabernacle.

Subsequently the priests brought the ark from the tent David had erected into the most holy place of Solomon's temple under the wings of the cherubim.

And it came to pass, when the priests were come out of the holy place, that the cloud filled the house of the LORD... 1 Kings 8:10 KJV

But alas, the sin of the Israelites would rise up again and a warning was issued. Sin always has consequences.

Therefore will I do unto this house, which is called by my name...as I have to Shiloh. Jeremiah 7:14 KJV

But before the temple would be destroyed, the presence of God departed.

Then the glory of the LORD departed from off the threshold of the house, and stood over the cherubim. Ezekiel 10:18 KJV

And the glory of the LORD went up from the midst of the city, and stood upon the mountain which is on the east side of the city. Ezekiel 11:23 KJV

The glory of the LORD departed from the Mount of Olives on the east side of the temple, the exact place where Christ will return.

And as forewarned, Jerusalem was besieged and the grand temple destroyed under the Babylonian king Nebuchadnezzar in 586 BC.

A meager attempt to rebuild Solomon's temple

The returning Jews from the captivity attempted to rebuild the temple in 536 BC, but it was a far cry from Solomon's original temple.

Then in 169 BC Antiochus Epiphanes desecrated the rebuilt temple.

In 20 BC Herod began restoring the temple remains. But the ark hadn't been seen since Solomon's temple was destroyed in 586 BC.

The temple was still being renovated under Herod during the time of Christ. It was a marvelous structure admired by all; however, it was being used for carnal purposes.

Remember during the early days of Jesus' ministry, He cleansed the temple of money changers. He told the Jews that they had turned His Father's house into a den of merchandise.

The Jews then asked Him by what authority He acted. They demanded a sign from Him to prove His authority.

Jesus answered, and said unto them, Destroy this temple, and in three days I will raise it up. John 2:19 KJV

The Jews chided Him and reminded Him that the renovation had been in progress for 46 years. Could He possibly raise it up in three days?

But he spoke of the temple of his body. John 2:21 KJV

Jesus was saying that He was the presence of God on earth. Even His disciples didn't comprehend His words until after His resurrection.

Shortly before Jesus was crucified, He and His disciples were visiting the temple admiring its splendor.

And Jesus said unto them, See ye not all these things? Verily I say unto you, There shall not be left here one stone upon another, that shall not be thrown down. Matthew 24:2 KJV

Approximately four decades later, the magnificent earthly temple was totally destroyed by the Roman general Titus, as forewarned by Jesus.

The unique presence of God after Jesus' departure

After Jesus' death, burial, resurrection, and ascension, He sent the Spirit of God to earth to dwell within His true followers.

Paul described this phenomenon.

Know ye not that ye are the temple of God, and that the Spirit of God dwelleth in you? 1 Corinthians 3:16 KJV

Therefore the presence of God was/is within His people.

Another physical temple is scheduled to be built

The next temple to be built after the destruction of the massive temple destroyed by the Romans in 70 AD would be built either just prior to the tribulation or during the first half of the tribulation.

This temple is referred to in Revelation 11. John was told to 'measure' the temple.

And there was given me a reed like a rod; and the angel stood, saying, Rise, and measure the temple of God, and the altar, and them that worship in it. Revelation 11:1 KJV

No measurements are given; however, the word 'measure' in this context means 'to number.' John was told to number the true worshippers, but omit the others who would subsequently persecute God's people.

It was at this time that the 'abomination of desolation' spoken of by Daniel would present himself as God in the temple and begin the last 3 ½ years called the 'great' tribulation.

And once again, Jesus had warned of that time prior to His crucifixion.

When ye, therefore, shall see the abomination of desolation, spoken of by Daniel the prophet, stand in the holy place...Then let them who are in Judea flee into the mountains...For then shall be great tribulation, such as was not since the beginning of the world to this time, no, nor ever shall be. Matthew 24:15-16, 21 KJV

Prepare for the greatest of all the earthly temples

Six centuries prior to the first advent of Jesus, the prophet Ezekiel told of a temple that would supersede both the temple destroyed in 70 AD and also the one to be built just prior to, or during, the first years of the tribulation.

The temple area described by Ezekiel would be one square mile.

"He measured the east side with the measuring rod (500 rods/reeds = 10.5 ft each)...He measured the north side...He measured the south side...He came around to the west side and measured... (all sides the same)" Ezekiel 42:16-19 NKJV

Within the temple area would be the holy place, measuring 60 ft x 30 ft, with the most holy place, measuring 30 ft x 30 ft, the same measurements of Solomon's temple.

The temple spoken of by Ezekiel would be occupied by the returning victorious Christ at the end of the great tribulation.

And the glory of the LORD came into the house by the way of the gate whose prospect is toward the east...and, behold, the glory of the LORD filled the house. Ezekiel 43:4-5 KJV

The prophet Haggai also looked past the temple which was destroyed in 70 AD, and the temple to be built before the tribulation temple, to the temple to be built for Christ when He returns to establish His millennial kingdom.

The glory of this latter house shall be greater than of the former, saith the LORD of hosts... Haggai 2:9 KJV

Jesus had spoken of the timing of this temple and His presence within it.

And Jesus said unto them, Verily I say unto you that ye who have followed me, in the regeneration, when the Son of Man shall sit on the throne of his glory, ye also shall

sit on twelve thrones, judging the twelve tribes of Israel.
Matthew 19:28 KJV

The timing for this event would be the beginning of the earthly Millennial Kingdom.

'Regeneration' in the present context is synonymous with 'restoration' and 'renewal.'

Jesus spoke of the 'restoration' before leaving the earth.

Peter confirms Jesus' words

After confirming the fulfillment of all things foretold by the prophets relative to Christ's suffering, Peter spoke of the future time of restoration.

But those things, which God before had shown by the mouth of all his prophets, that Christ should suffer, he hath so fulfilled. Acts 3:18 KJV

Christ had assured His disciples that they could have the same confidence that the other prophecies spoken by the prophets would be fulfilled in like manner.

After Peter healed the lame man in the name of Jesus Christ, he preached repentance in preparation of the return of Jesus.

Repent, therefore, and be converted, that your sins may be blotted out, when the times of refreshing shall come from

*the presence of the Lord; and he shall send Jesus Christ,
who before was preached unto you, whom the heaven must
receive until the times of restitution of all things, which God
hath spoken by the mouth of all his holy prophets since the
age (world) began.* Acts 3:19-21 KJV

'Refreshing' means 'rest' and 'peace.'

Jesus had revealed the sequence of events which would
follow His death, resurrection, and ascension. Christ would
be at the right hand of His Father until He is sent back to
restore all things at the end of the tribulation.

The phrase 'all things' means those things spoken by
the prophets and saints.

'Restitution' is from the Greek *apokatastasis* meaning
'to return something to its former condition.'

And when the phrase 'since the age (world) began,' is
used, it is from the Greek *aion* meaning 'time,' instead
of *kosmos* which means the order of civilization on the
inhabited earth.

What about the Ark of the Covenant?

A question dating back many years will be addressed,
i.e. will the Ark of the Covenant be found in the millennial
temple?

Recall, the original tabernacle and Solomon's temple
focused on the Ark of the Covenant; however, the ark was

not included in the rebuilt temple after the 70 year captivity, nor was it included in Herod's temple at the time of Christ.

The ark was taken, and possible destroyed, by Nebuchadnezzar when he besieged the city of Jerusalem and the temple in 586 BC.

And it shall come to pass, when ye are multiplied and increased in the land, in those days, saith the LORD, they shall say no more, The ark of the covenant of the LORD; neither shall it come to mind, neither shall they remember it, neither shall they miss it, neither shall that be done any more. At that time they shall call Jerusalem the throne of the LORD... Jeremiah 3:16-17a KJV

There will no longer be a 'representation of God,' He will be in the presence of redeemed man throughout eternity, as it was in the beginning.

This temple will remain for 1,000 years; however, this is not the end of the story.

The ultimate, eternal presence of God

The millennial temple as described by Ezekiel will be the final temple on earth constructed by man; however, that temple is just the precursor to God's ultimate, eternal presence on earth.

The tabernacle and temples described thus far have just been representations of the true heavenly temple.

After Christ's ascension, He as High Priest returned to the true, heavenly sanctuary.

...who is seated on the right hand of the throne of the Majesty in the heavens, a minister of the sanctuary, and of the true tabernacle, which the Lord pitched, and not man. Hebrews 8:1b-2 KJV

The heavenly, i.e. true tabernacle was the pattern for the earthly tabernacle and subsequent temples.

Recall, John stated in the final book of the Bible, that he would be shown things that must take place after the church age.

At that point the tribulation period is described in detail as well as the millennial period which follows. After the great white throne judgment, the ultimate presence of God is introduced.

New heavens and new earth

The prophet Isaiah spoke of that wondrous promise more than two millennia ago.

For, behold, I create new heavens and a new earth, and the former shall not be remembered, nor come into mind. But be glad and rejoice forever in that which I create; for, behold, I create Jerusalem a rejoicing... Isaiah 65:17-18 KJV

It is significant that 'new' in the present context is the Hebrew *chadash* which means 'fresh' and 'renewed.'

It is the same word used in the following.

For as the new heavens and the new earth, which I will make, shall remain before me, saith the LORD, so shall your seed and your name remain. Isaiah 66:22 KJV

The physical planet will survive the fiery judgment as it did during the flood in the time of Noah.

The doomsday prognosticators should rethink their fears about the need to migrate to another planet, believing earth will be destroyed.

The renewal process will require that the present curse must be removed, and so it will be.

Deliverance from the curse

The concept of deliverance was also spoken previously by the apostles.

"For the earnest expectation of the creation eagerly waits for the revealing of the sons of God. For the creation was subjected to futility...the creation itself also will be delivered from the bondage of corruption into the glorious liberty of the children of God." Romans 8:19-21 NKJV

'Futility' means the inability to fulfill God's purpose for earth or man while under the curse; while 'delivered' means to be 'released' or 'set free.'

The term 'bondage of corruption' means that the elements of the new heaven and earth will not be subject to decay.

Consider also:

"Then comes the end, when He delivers the kingdom to God the Father, when He puts an end to all rule and all authority and power. For He must reign till He has put all enemies under His feet...Now when all things are made subject to Him, then the Son Himself will also be subject to Him who put all things under Him, that God may be all in all."
1 Corinthians 15:24-25, 28 NKJV

The Father has delegated all things to His Son, and when all things are restored, the Son will once again be subject to the Father.

*And there shall be no more curse...*Revelation 22:3 KJV

Enter New Jerusalem

The apostle John was given a vision confirming Isaiah's prophecy.

*And I saw a new heaven and a new earth; for the first heaven and the first earth were passed away...*Revelation 21:1 KJV

'New' from the Greek *kainos* likewise means 'qualitatively new,' or 'renewed.'

And I, John, saw the holy city new Jerusalem, coming down from God out of heaven...And I heard a great voice out of heaven saying, Behold, the tabernacle of God is with men, and he will dwell with them... Revelation 21:2-3 KJV

'City' in this context essentially means a city enclosed with a wall, i.e. a walled town. Interestingly, the antonym for this city is *kosmos*, or the world.

Shortly thereafter an angel provided further details of the city.

And the city lieth foursquare, and the length is as large as the breadth; and he measured the city with the reed, twelve thousand furlongs. The length and the breadth and the height of it are equal. Revelation 21:16 KJV

Twelve thousand furlongs is approximately equivalent to 1,400 miles.

Thus the city is a perfect cube, i.e. length, width, and height are equal exactly like the dimensions of the most holy place in the tabernacle and temples!

But something seemed to be lacking in the city.

And I saw no temple in it; for the Lord God Almighty and the Lamb are the temple of it. Revelation 21:22 KJV

The city is the temple

And he showed me a pure river of water of life, clear as crystal, proceeding out of the throne of God and of the Lamb. Revelation 22:1 KJV

In the midst of the street of it, and on either side of the river, was there the tree of life, which bore twelve kinds of fruits, and yielded her fruit every month; and the leaves of the tree were for the healing of the nations. Revelation 22:2 KJV

And they shall see his face; and his name shall be in their foreheads. Revelation 22:4 KJV

Now let's go back to see how it was in the beginning for man.

"The LORD God planted a garden eastward in Eden, and there He put the man whom He had formed (created). And out of the ground the LORD God made every tree grow that is pleasant to the sight and good for food. The tree of life was also in the midst of the garden...Now a river went out of Eden to water the garden..." Genesis 2:8-10 NKJV

Thus in the beginning man had trees that bore fruit for food; there was a river to water the garden; the tree of life was in the garden; and man was in the very presence of God.

Therefore, key words found in God's incomprehensible and immutable plan for His highest creation include:

- Return

- Repent

- Redeem

- Renew

- Restore

The thing that hath been, it is that which shall be; and that which is done, is that which shall be done; and there is no new thing under the sun. Is there any thing whereof it may be said, See, this is new? It hath been already of old time, which was before us. Ecclesiastes 1:9-10 KJV

Chapter 2

Return and Repent

Inasmuch as 'return and repent' are the initial steps in the ultimate restoration of heaven and earth, we'll focus on those two words in this chapter. And recall both return and repent can only occur after God's proactive grace.

Webster agrees with the basic definition of numerous 're' words used in Scripture. The basic idea of the prefix 're' means 'again,' or 'to go back.'

To begin with we'll focus on the Old Testament use of the Hebrew word *Shuv*. *Shuv* has numerous synonyms including turn back, return, reverse, again, restore, or move back to the point of departure.

The context of the following passage speaks of Israel's future glory after they return to God following centuries of disobedience and dispersion.

"Now it shall come to pass, when all these things come upon you, the blessing and the curse which I have set before you, and you call them to mind...and you return to the

LORD your God and obey His voice...that the LORD your God will bring you back from captivity...and gather you again from all the nations where the LORD your God has scattered you." Deuteronomy 30:1-3 NKJV

The following phrases found in the above passage are translated from the Hebrew word *Shuv.*

...call them to mind...
...and you return to the LORD...
...the LORD will bring you back...
...gather you again...

God will in the future bless Israel beyond measure if they will obey and 'turn to the LORD your God,' or repent, i.e. return to their point of departure from His commandments and statutes.

...If thou shalt hearken unto the voice of the LORD thy God, to keep his commandments and his statutes...and if thou turn unto the LORD thy God with all thine heart, and with all thy soul. Deuteronomy 30:10 KJV

And Israel will only be able to repent by the proactive grace of the Holy Spirit.

...I will put my law in their inward parts, and write it in their hearts, and will be their God, and they shall be my people. Jeremiah 31:33b KJV

Now inasmuch as all that happened to Israel was 'written for our admonition, upon which the ends of the ages have come,' let's explore more relative to the foundational doctrine of repentance.

Solomon spoke of the blessings awaiting those who return to God

Let's progress 450 years from Deuteronomy to the days of King Solomon and see if anything had changed. The time would be approximately 961 BC when Solomon dedicated the magnificent temple he had just completed.

In his dedication prayer, Solomon spoke the following on behalf of the people:

"When they sin against You (for there is no one who does not sin)...yet when they come to themselves...and when they return to You with all their heart...then hear in heaven... their prayer...and forgive..." 1 Kings 8:46-50 NKJV

The phrase 'when they come to themselves' is expressed by one word, 'bethink,' in the KJ which means 'to remember,' or to contemplate things of the past. The word 'bethink' is once again from the basic Hebrew *Shuv*. And 'return' in the above means repent from the same Hebrew base word.

Thus the above passage states that the people would sin, and then would think about their blessings prior to their sin.

Then when they returned to God (repented) they would be forgiven.

After the dedication of Solomon's temple, God appeared to Solomon a second time and reaffirmed the great truth regarding sin, repentance, and forgiveness.

Then the LORD appeared to Solomon at night and said... "If I shut up the heavens so that there is no rain, or if I command the locust to devour the land, or if I send pestilence among My people, and My people who are called by My name humble themselves and pray, and seek My face and turn from their wicked ways, than I will hear from heaven, and forgive their sin, and will heal their land."
2 Chronicles 7:12-14 NASB

God said that He would chastise Israel for their wicked ways. However, after the necessary chastisement, if His people would acknowledge their sin with humble hearts and turn (repent) from their wicked ways, God would forgive them.

Sin, chastisement, and humble repentance are followed by redemption and forgiveness.

Solomon's wisdom will be reaffirmed throughout all ages.

Repentance according to the prophets

The prophets were prominent in Israel's history from approximately 850 BC to 420 BC.

The prophets had much to say about returning to God.

Let the wicked forsake his way, and the unrighteous man his thoughts, and let him return unto the LORD, and he will have mercy upon him...for he will abundantly pardon. Isaiah 55:7 KJV

Sin is described as both actions and thoughts. Such wickedness must be recognized and forsaken. And then the sinner must return to the LORD, i.e. repent, and he shall be forgiven.

It is confirmed that the sequence had not changed, nor will it. The sinner must return to where he was before forsaking the word of God.

God desires His children to repent and return to Him, and He will go to great lengths with longsuffering to bring them back to Himself.

Ezekiel spoke of Israel's refusal to give up idols, along with the required consequences.

"Therefore say to the house of Israel...'Repent, turn away from your idols...for anyone of the house of Israel... who separates himself from Me and sets up his idols...I will set My face against that man and make him a sign and a proverb, and I will cut him off from the midst of my people...'" Ezekiel 14:6-8 NKJV

Again, God invites those involved with idols to turn away (repent) from such. Then He describes the consequences of not repenting.

Another example.

Nevertheless, if thou warn the wicked of his way to turn from it, if he do not turn from his way, he shall die in his iniquity...Say unto them, As I live, saith the Lord God, I have no pleasure in the death of the wicked, but that the wicked turn from his way and live; turn ye, turn from your evil ways; for why will ye die, O house of Israel?
Ezekiel 33:9, 11 KJV

God pleads for His people to turn (repent) confirming the necessary consequence of death.

Zechariah then speaks of God's anger towards the ancestors of the current generation.

Thus saith the LORD of hosts, Turn unto me, saith the LORD...Be not as your fathers, unto whom the former prophets have cried, saying...Turn now from you evil ways, and from your evil doings; but they did not hear, nor hearken unto me... Zechariah 1:3-4 KJV

And then the final message from the last Old Testament prophet.

For I am the LORD, I change not...Even from the days of your fathers ye are gone away from mine ordinances,

31

and have not kept them. Return unto me, and I will return unto you... Malachi 3:6-7 KJV

Thus all have sinned; thus all need to turn from their ways (repent), which can only be done through the Holy Spirit. True repentance and a contrite heart will be a sweet savor to a Holy God who will forgive graciously.

True repentance is the gospel message

A significant Greek word for repentance is *metanoeo* which means not only regret or remorse, but it also means genuine sorrow accompanied by a true change of heart driven by the Holy Spirit. Therefore genuine repentance transcends pious sorrow and leads one to the gospel of Jesus Christ.

It is very significant that this type of repentance is accompanied by *epistrepho* which means to come back, i.e. a turn about.

Recall, the basic meaning of 're' words includes 'again,' or to turn back to the point before abandoning God's words.

Repentance was the message of John the Baptist

In those days came John the Baptist, preaching in the wilderness of Judea, and saying, Repent; for the kingdom of heaven is at hand. For this is he that was spoken of by the prophet, Isaiah... Matthew 3:1-3a KJV

The Pharisees and Sadducees were curious and came to John, but John saw right through their hypocrisy and motives.

The Pharisees and Sadducees were aware of the coming wrath in the day of the Lord, but they thought their relationship to Abraham was sufficient to save them.

Bring forth, therefore, fruits befitting repentance, and think not to say within yourselves, We have Abraham as our father... Matthew 3:8-9a KJV

John boldly told them that true repentance required a change of heart and actions. Their ancestry alone could not save them from the wrath to come.

Subsequently, due to John's boldness and lack of political correctness, he was put in prison and executed.

Now after John was put in prison, Jesus came into Galilee, preaching the gospel of the kingdom of God, and saying, The time is fulfilled, and the kingdom of God is at hand, repent, and believe the gospel. Mark 1:14-15 KJV

Jesus was the object of John's message, and Jesus picked up where John left off. Immediately after the devil unsuccessfully tempted Jesus, Jesus began His ministry.

Repentance was the early message of Jesus

From that time Jesus began to preach, and to say, Repent; for the kingdom of heaven is at hand. Matthew 4:17 KJV

Shortly thereafter, Jesus called out the twelve and sent them out two by two to present the gospel message.

And they went out, and preached that men should repent. Mark 6:12 KJV

Note again that the message of repentance preceded the gospel message.

Jesus firmly rebuked those who rejected His call to repentance.

The Pharisees continued their refusal to heed the truth and requested a sign from Jesus to prove his authority.

Then certain of the scribes and of the Pharisees answered, saying, Master, we would see a sign from thee. Matthew 12:38 KJV

Jesus responded that the sign of Jonah was sufficient to prove His authenticity. The city of Nineveh repented due to Jonah's message. Jesus would fulfill the story of Jonah by spending three days and three nights in the heart of the earth. Even the wickedness of Nineveh was less than the wickedness of the current generation.

The men of Nineveh shall rise in judgment with this generation, and shall condemn it; because they repented at the preaching of Jonah; and, behold, a greater than Jonah is here. Matthew 12:41 KJV

After His resurrection Jesus' last words prior to His ascension stressed the necessity of repentance.

...Thus it is written, and thus it behooved Christ to suffer, and to rise from the dead the third day; and that repentance and remission of sins should be preached in his name among all nations, beginning at Jerusalem.
Luke 24:46-47 KJV

Indeed, Jesus taught that repentance was an integral part of the gospel message and, in fact, the initial step in the salvation process initiated by God.

Peter teaches repentance in the early church

Shortly after Jesus' ascension, Peter, being filled with the Spirit, delivered a bold sermon to the crowd in Jerusalem who were celebrating the Day of Pentecost.

Many Jews took Peter's message to heart and asked him what they should do at this point.

Then Peter said unto them, Repent, and be baptized, every one of you, in the name of Jesus Christ for the remission of sins, and ye shall receive the gift of the Holy Spirit. Acts 2:38 KJV

The Jews were instructed to repent by humbly acknowledging their sin and being totally immersed in Christ as evidenced by their heart-felt actions. Their repentance would confirm the work and presence of the Holy Spirit.

As a result of Peter's revelations, about 3,000 souls were saved that day and became part of the first church.

Peter's message was that true repentance is followed by forgiveness of sins and the gift of the Holy Spirit.

In his epistles addressed to Christians dispersed throughout present day Turkey, Peter continued to speak of the significance of repentance. After denouncing false teachers he reinforced God's promises for the future.

The Lord is not slack concerning his promise...but is longsuffering toward us, not willing that any should perish, but that all should come to repentance. 2 Peter 3:9 KJV

Peter's message was that repentance was a necessary step in salvation. God's longsuffering confirms that He does not immediately deal with one's sin, but will give that person time to repent and accept that his sin was paid for on the cross.

Teaching of repentance remained one of the most important aspects of the gospel message through the ages.

Paul also taught the doctrine of repentance to the fledgling church

After his admonishment to the church at Corinth for their ungodly thinking and practices, Paul steadfastly prayed for their repentance. Paul knew that his previous letter had caused them sorrow. He himself had regrets for a short time for causing their grief; however, their grief led to repentance.

Now I rejoice, not that ye were made sorry but that ye sorrowed to repentance; for ye were made sorry after a godly manner...For godly sorrow worketh repentance to salvation... 2 Corinthians 7:9-10a KJV

Paul rejoiced that the truth and steadfastness to the word of God led to repentance to a needful church. Sorrow induced by the Holy Spirit leads to true repentance, not worldly repentance.

Paul prepared Timothy by teaching him the doctrine of repentance

As Paul was instructing Timothy, he gave godly advice on how to deal with unbelievers with the goal of leading them to salvation.

Timothy was to avoid foolish disputes, which produce nothing.

And the servant of the Lord must not strive, but be gentle unto all men, apt to teach, patient, in meekness instructing those that oppose him, if God, perhaps, will give them repentance to the acknowledging of the truth...
2 Timothy 2:24-25 KJV

That message has remained relevant through the ages. God uses His servants to prepare the unbelieving to receive the gift of repentance. Godly repentance is the truth versus the deceit of the devil.

In his letter to Christians in Rome Paul compares pious man's judgment of one's fellows with the gracious riches of God. Such a one does not know or understand the sovereignty of God. God is the initiator of one's repentance.

Or despisest thou the riches of his goodness and forbearance and long-suffering, not knowing that the goodness of God leadeth thee to repentance? Romans 2:4 KJV

The message remains the same, i.e. true repentance, or change of heart, is only accomplished by the working of the Holy Spirit.

Paul also taught repentance to gentile leaders

At a later time the converted Apostle Paul spoke to a crowd of Greeks at Mars Hill. He acknowledged that they were very religious. Then he addressed their object of worship which they referred to as 'The Unknown God.'

As would be expected, Paul enlightened their understanding. He explained that their 'unknown God' was in fact the God of the universe. He then expounded on their duty based on the new revelations.

And the times of this ignorance God overlooked, but now commandeth all men everywhere to repent, because he hath appointed a day, in which he will judge the world in righteousness by that man whom he hath ordained; concerning which he hath given assurance unto all men in that he hath raised him from the dead. Acts 17:30-31 KJV

Paul explained that true repentance is necessary in order to escape the judgment to come, which was confirmed by Jesus' resurrection.

Once again it is confirmed that the first step in the salvation process is repentance. Such heart-felt contrition would produce works befitting a changed heart. And remember, a changed heart is the result of the working of the Holy Spirit.

The fate of the non-repentant

But those who judge their fellow men and are unwilling to receive repentance will face God's wrath.

But after thy hardness and impenitent heart treasurest up unto thyself wrath against the day of wrath and revelation of the righteous judgment of God, who will render to every man according to his deeds... Romans 2:5 KJV

'Impenitent' in the above verse means 'without repentance or change of heart.' A hard heart leads to God's required wrath.

Jesus' words to the churches in the Book of Revelation stresses the need to repent. The sad truth is, however, that the majority of mankind will reject God's gracious gift.

After the middle of Daniel's 70th week, after the seven seals are opened and the sixth trumpet sounds which kills a third of mankind, the majority are still unwilling to repent.

And the rest of the men who were not killed by these plagues yet repented not of the works of their hands, that they should not worship demons, and idols of gold, and silver...neither repented they of their murders, nor of their sorceries, nor of their fornication, nor of their thefts. Revelation 9:20-21 KJV

Things will get progressively worse, so that even after the fifth bowl of darkness and pain is poured out on the final world kingdom, men will not repent, instead:

And blasphemed the God of heaven because of their pains and their sores, and repented not of their deeds. Revelation 16:11 KJV

Non-repentance has its price.

Invalid Repentance

Another significant Greek word translated 'repentance' in the New Testament is *metamelomai* which not only means 'repent,' but also means 'regret.'

The problem; however, is that this type of regret is the fear of the consequence of one's sin.

'Metamelomai' does not include the basic change in a person resulting from the power of the Holy Spirit. It is simply a human decision to avoid sin's consequences.

Jesus warned of this type of shallow repentance.

Not every one that saith unto me, Lord, Lord, shall enter into the kingdom of heaven, but he that doeth the will of my Father, who is in heaven. Matthew 7:21 KJV

True repentance involves a basic change in the person who not only hears the word of God, but puts those words into action.

Therefore, whosoever heareth these sayings of mine, and doeth them, I will liken him unto a wise man, who built his house upon a rock. And the rain descended, and the floods came, and the winds blew and beat upon that house, and it fell not; for it was founded upon a rock. Matthew 7:24-25 KJV

Likewise, the one who only hears God's word, without acting on it, will build his house on the sand; and his house will fall when the wind and rain comes.

Jesus taught that tax collectors and sinners heard and repented, while the Pharisees and lawyers heard and scoffed.

"And when all the people heard Him, even the tax collectors justified (declared the righteousness of) God, having been baptized with the baptism of John. But the Pharisees and lawyers rejected the will of God for themselves, not having been baptized by him." Luke 7:29-30 NKJV

The self righteous do not see the need to repent

Jesus subsequently taught that the majority would consider themselves to be self righteous and not be in need of true repentance.

The self righteous believe they are safe; they have been deceived by thinking that 'religion' or good deeds are sufficient to have favor with God.

Jesus used the parable of the two sons to illustrate to the chief priests and elders true repentance.

"...A man had two sons, and he came to the first and said, 'Son, go, work today in my vineyard.' He answered and said, 'I will not,' but afterward he regretted it and went. Then he came to the second and said likewise. And he answered and said, 'I go, sir,' but he did not go. Which of the two did the will of his father?" Matthew 21:28-30 NKJV

When Jesus asked the Jewish leaders which of the two sons did the will of their father, they answered correctly that the first son did their father's will.

At that point Jesus called out their hypocrisy.

...Verily I say unto you that the tax collectors and the harlots go into the kingdom of God before you. For John came unto you in the way of righteousness, and ye believed him not; but the tax collectors and the harlots believed him; and ye, when ye had seen it, repented not afterward, that ye might believe him. Matthew 21:31b-32 KJV

Does God really 'repent?'

There are two primary Hebrew words used in the Old Testament meaning 'repent.'

The Hebrew word attributable to God's repentance is *Nacham,* meaning a change of heart, mind, or purpose resulting from experiencing sorrow, pity, or preparing to take revenge.

The first reference attributed to God's repentance is found in the early chapters of Genesis when the universal wickedness of man was noted.

And God saw that the wickedness of man was great in the earth...and it repented the LORD that he had made man on the earth...and the LORD said, I will destroy man whom I have created from the face of the earth... Genesis 6:5-7 KJV

Several thousand years later Moses pleaded for God to repent of His judgment of destruction on the Israelites after they had molded the golden calf.

God's response?

And the LORD repented of the evil which he thought to do unto his people. Exodus 32:14 KJV

Eight hundred years passed to the time of Jeremiah the prophet. God spoke to Jeremiah relative to His sovereignty over Israel.

If that nation, against whom I have pronounced, turn from their evil, I will repent of the evil that I thought to do unto them. Jeremiah 18:8 KJV

Shortly thereafter, God again told Jeremiah to speak to Israel about their behavior and God's reaction.

Therefore, now amend your ways and your doings, and obey the voice of the LORD, your God, and the LORD will repent him of the evil that he hath pronounced against you. Jeremiah 26:13 KJV

Thus, it appears that God's actions or inactions are contingent on Israel's obedience or disobedience to God's commandments.

The truth

But let's take a closer look at reality. To do this we'll borrow a definition from Webster. The specific definition to be examined is the word *anthropopathisma* which means to attribute human feelings and emotions to that which is not human. It is used metaphorically in the Bible to ascribe human emotions to God.

Therefore, it may appear that God changes His mind in response to man's actions, but is that really possible? Again, the Scriptures provide the answer.

God is not a man, that he should lie; neither the son of man, that he should repent. Hath he said, and shall he not do it? Or hath he spoken, and shall he not make it good? Numbers 23:19 KJV

God's plan for His chosen was devised from the foundation of the world and is immutable.

A great summation is found in the book of Isaiah.

Remember the former things of old; for I am God, and there is none else...declaring the end from the beginning, and from ancient times the things that are not yet done, saying, My counsel shall stand, and I will do all my pleasure...Yea, I have spoken it, I will also bring it to pass; I have purposed it, I will also do it. Isaiah 46:9-11 KJV

Therefore, God does not change His mind or His plan to react to what man does; on the contrary God has spoken in advance what man would think and do.

Chapter 3

Redemption Follows Repentance

Redemption is perhaps the key doctrine in the Bible. Redemption is also initiated by an act of God. After genuine repentance has taken place, redemption is accomplished, which leads to forgiveness and restoration.

There are two major Hebrew words used in the Old Testament which define redemption. The word to be used initially is *Gaal*. There are several significant synonyms that are based on *Gaal* including but not limited to ransom, release, deliver, purchase, and kinsman.

The main idea of *Gaal* is to buy something back. That means that redemption is not only 'from' something, but 'to' something. And like the other 're' words we're studying, the 'to something' means a change of position or status; however, the change reverts back to where something was before redemption was required.

Redemption applied

The Bible presents excellent examples describing the significance of redemption. A major premise is that everything and everyone belongs to God.

Initially for Israel, nearly everything and everyone sold for whatever reason could be redeemed by a kinsman for a price. If not redeemed, the property or person would automatically be returned to the designated owner at the year of Jubilee.

The initial example to be examined describes the redemption of physical property.

And in all the land of your possession ye shall grant a redemption for the land. If thy brother hath become poor, and hath sold away some of his possession, and if any of his kin come to redeem it, then shall he redeem that which his brother sold. Leviticus 25:24-25 KJV

The above reveals that there are basically three key ingredients in the redemption phenomena, i.e. a lost possession, a price necessary to buy the lost possession back, and a near relative (kinsman) willing to pay the price to buy the lost possession back.

And remember, the lost possession could be property, an individual redeemed from slavery, or an entire nation.

The topic of redemption is very detailed. In one of our previous books entitled: ***God's Plan for His Chosen*** there are separate chapters dedicated to defining lost possessions, redemptive price, and kinsman redeemers.

Redemption for national Israel

While Israel was still under Egyptian bondage, God spoke to Moses.

Wherefore say unto the children of Israel, I am the LORD, and I will bring you out from under the burdens of the Egyptians, and I will rid you out of their bondage, and I will redeem you with an outstretched arm, and with great judgments; and I will take you to me for a people...and ye shall know that I am the LORD your God... Exodus 6:6-7 KJV

At that time God announced that He would be Israel's Redeemer and deliver them from Egyptian bondage. Redemption for Israel would also include judgment for their oppressors who refused to free them. Notice all the 'I wills' after God confirms that He is the LORD.

Then after Israel was freed from bondage, Moses acknowledged that their freedom was a gracious act of God.

Thou in thy mercy hast led forth the people whom thou hast redeemed; thou hast guided them in thy strength unto thy holy habitation. Exodus 15:13 KJV

Approximately 435 years later when David received the everlasting promises of God for an eternal kingdom, he acknowledged his God as the Redeemer of Israel.

And what one nation in the earth is like thy people, even like Israel, whom God went to redeem for a people to himself, and to make him a name, and to do for you great things and awe-inspiring, for thy land, before thy people, which thou redeemedst to thee from Egypt, from the nations and their gods? For thou has confirmed to thyself thy people, Israel, to be a people unto thee forever...
2 Samuel 7:23-24 KJV

In this verse David used the Hebrew *Padhah* which includes the meaning of *Gaal*, but it further means to release from servitude and the accompanying transfer of ownership by paying the redemptive price.

The psalmist then recounts Israel's history of disobedience and yet God's redemptive mercy.

"We have sinned with our fathers...Our fathers in Egypt did not understand Your wonders; they did not remember the multitude of Your mercies, but rebelled by the Red Sea...Nevertheless He saved them for His name's sake... and redeemed them from the hand of the enemy..."
Psalm 106:6-8, 10 NKJV

Israel's redemption is confirmed by the prophets

The following will continue the discussion of redemption using the same Hebrew word *Gaal*. Scripture references will focus on national Israel and her capital city Jerusalem.

But, now, thus saith the LORD who created thee, O Jacob, and he who formed thee, O Israel, Fear not; for I have redeemed thee, I have called thee by thy name; thou art mine. Isaiah 43:1 KJV

Israel is indeed God's chosen nation. He redeemed Israel out of Egypt and subsequently out of Babylon. He will in the future redeem them out of all nations to be His glory forever in the land He promised Abraham several millennia earlier.

Isaiah then states that God has/will blot out all of Israel's sins and redeem them. Again, final redemption for Israel will be after Daniel's 70th week.

I have blotted out, like a thick cloud, thy transgressions, and, like a cloud, thy sins; return unto me; for I have redeemed thee. Sing, O ye heavens; for the LORD hath done it; shout, ye lower parts of the earth...for the LORD hath redeemed Jacob, and glorified himself in Israel. Isaiah 44:22-23 KJV

Israel's final redemption is spoken of in the past tense; i.e. it is a sure thing. Israel's sins had to be dealt with and forgiven before redemption was done. And again it is stressed that God is glorified in Israel.

Israel's redemption, past, present, and future, was ordained from the foundation of the world

"I have declared the former things from the beginning... Listen to Me, O Jacob, and Israel, My called: I am He, I am the First, I am also the Last. Indeed My hand has laid the foundation of the earth...Thus says the LORD, your Redeemer...'I am the LORD your God...Go forth from Babylon! Utter it to the end of the earth;' Say, 'The LORD had redeemed His servant Jacob!'" Isaiah 48:3a, 12-13, 17, 20 NKJV

This passage has both short-term and long-term implication.

God confirms again that Israel is His chosen nation; He confirms His deity; He proclaims that He is Israel's Redeemer, and would soon deliver them from Babylon. He instructs Israel to tell all nations that their God has redeemed and delivered them once again from bondage.

Israel was/is metaphorically wed to God

Next God describes His relationship with Israel as He being her husband and she being a forsaken wife.

"For your Maker is your husband...and your Redeemer is the Holy One of Israel; He is called the God of the whole

earth...For a mere moment I have forsaken you...with a little wrath I hid My face from you...but with everlasting kindness I will have mercy on you, says the LORD, your Redeemer." Isaiah 54:5, 7-8 NKJV

God acknowledges that He forsook His wife for a very short time because of her unfaithfulness; however, as her Husband and Redeemer, He would return to her with everlasting kindness.

Israel's apostasy had caused them grave hardship. But Israel had temporarily come to their senses and owned up to their sin. With truly penitent hearts they prayed:

...Thou, O LORD, art our father, our redeemer; thy name is from everlasting. Isaiah 63:16b KJV

Thus God was not only Israel's Redeemer, He also loved them as a husband and as a father, and He had done so from everlasting.

Redemption for Jerusalem

And then Isaiah records God's redemption of Israel's everlasting capital, i.e. Jerusalem.

Jerusalem had become very rich and subsequently very proud. She prostituted herself to other nations for her wealth.

For thus saith the LORD, Ye have sold yourselves for nothing, and ye shall be redeemed without money.
Isaiah 52:3 KJV

And the Redeemer shall come to Zion, and unto those who turn from transgression in Jacob, saith the LORD.
Isaiah 59:20 KJV

Behold, the LORD hath proclaimed unto the end of the earth: Say ye to the daughter of Zion, Behold, thy salvation cometh...and they shall call them, The holy people, The redeemed of the LORD... Isaiah 62:11-12 KJV

Remember, God has proclaimed that Jerusalem would be Israel's capital throughout eternity.

What other nation or capital city has such rich promises as Israel and Jerusalem? There is no other, and yet Israel is hated above all nations, and Jerusalem has been disqualified as Israel's capital by the United Nations. Go figure.

Redemption for the individual

We've considered redemption based on the Hebrew word *Gaal* which meant ransom, release, and deliver, owing to a kinsman redeemer paying the redemptive price. The main idea of *Gaal* was to buy back something that had been lost.

Now let's look at redemption based on the Hebrew word *Padhah* which was introduced earlier. Recall, *Padhah* adds to *Gaal* to include the release from servitude and the accompanying transfer of ownership by paying the redemptive price.

Padhah is used to describe the immaterial part of man, i.e. the soul.

And the LORD God formed man of the dust of the ground, and breathed into his nostrils the breath of life; and man became a living soul (being). Genesis 2:7 KJV

Soul means the inner person, including the spirit and mind; the very essence of one's being. Soul is synonymous with breath which in turn is synonymous with wind and spirit.

When David was king he addressed the two who had killed Saul's replacement Ishbosheth, thinking they had done a favor for David.

David sternly rebuked their reasoning.

And David answered...and said unto them, As the LORD liveth, who hath redeemed my soul out of all adversity... 2 Samuel 4:9 KJV

David acknowledged that his thinking now surpassed the reasoning of natural man. The two who attempted to impress others with worldly wisdom had their hands and feet severed and were hung.

The Psalmist confirmed that one's soul was preserved even in death if that soul had been redeemed.

But God will redeem my soul from the power of sheol; for He shall receive me. Psalm 49:15 KJV

David confirmed the redemption of the soul of the righteous.

Evil shall slay the wicked, and they that hate the righteous shall be desolate. The LORD redeemeth the soul of his servants; and none of them who trust in him shall be desolate. Psalm 34:21-22 KJV

Of profound significance is the fact that only God can redeem one's soul. The best of men are totally impotent to redeem himself or his brother.

None of them can by any means redeem his brother, nor give to God a ransom for him (for the redemption of their soul is precious...) Psalm 49:7-8 KJV

Redemption in the church age

There are five predominant Greek words used to define redemption in the New Testament. All five share common synonymous words and phrases:

1) to purchase for a price, or pay a ransom

2) to deliver, release, or set free

3) to take possession of and declare ownership

4) to give atonement, reconciliation, justification, and glorification

5) the Kinsman Redeemer is Christ, and the required payment is His innocent blood

The New Testament declares that the redemption provided by Christ was originally for Israel. However, the Old Covenant was not sufficient for Israel's redemption.

Christ's blood was the redemptive price for both Israel and the church

Subsequently, the writer of the Book of Hebrews confirmed that redemption to be given to the church was also sufficient to fulfill for Israel what the Old Covenant could not do.

After the inability of the blood of animals to remit sins was declared, the writer states:

...How much more shall the blood of Christ, who through the eternal Spirit offered himself without spot to God, purge your conscience from dead works to serve the living God? And for this cause he is the mediator of the new testament (covenant), that by means of death, for the redemption of the transgressions that were under the first testament (covenant)... Hebrews 9:14-15 KJV

Another significant confirmation in the New Testament was that redemption included both body and soul.

...but ourselves also, who have the first fruits of the Spirit...waiting for the adoption, that is, the redemption of our body. Romans 8:23 KJV

The truth of bodily redemption was also explained to the church at Ephesus. As Paul was revealing the character of the redeemed, he spoke of the future day of redemption.

Christ's shed blood assured future glorification of the redeemed

And grieve not the Holy Spirit of God, by whom ye are sealed unto the day of redemption. Ephesians 4:30 KJV

The future day of redemption refers to the resurrection and glorification of all believers at the return of Christ, their Kinsman Redeemer.

And Paul explains that future glorification is guaranteed.

"In Him also we have obtained an inheritance, being predestined according to the purpose of Him who works all things according to the counsel of His will...In Him... having believed...you were sealed with the Holy Spirit of promise, who is the guarantee of our inheritance until the redemption of the purchased possession..."
Ephesians 1:11, 13 NKJV

Christ's shed blood was sufficient to redeem the entire creation

Paul revealed that redemption offered by Christ would affect the entire creation which had been cursed (subjected to futility) due to the fall in the garden, however:

...the creation itself also shall be delivered from the bondage of corruption into the glorious liberty of the children of God. For we know that the whole creation groaneth and travaileth in pain together until now. Romans 8:21-22 KJV

Therefore, the lost possession was a corrupted earth, and loss of life for mankind was part of the curse.

The only qualified Kinsman Redeemer was the God/ Man Jesus Christ.

And the only acceptable redemptive price was the blood of Christ.

All believers anxiously await perhaps the most beautiful words in the Bible describing the New Jerusalem.

*And there shall be no more curse, but the throne of God and of the Lamb shall be in it...*Revelation 22:3 KJV

Redemption frees one from the curse of the law

Another significant aspect of redemption is that the redeemed is no longer under the curse of the law which no one could fully obey.

Christ hath redeemed us from the curse of the law, being made a curse for us...that the blessing of Abraham might come on the Gentiles through Jesus Christ...
Galatians 3:13-14 KJV

Jesus redeemed the church from the curse of the law by taking on Himself the curse by perfectly fulfilling the law so that the church could share in the blessings promised to Abraham's seed.

Paul then provided more detail relative to Christ and the law.

Even so we, when we were children, were in bondage under the elements of the world. But, when the fullness of the time had come, God sent forth His Son, made of a woman, made under the law, to redeem them that were under the law, that we might receive the adoption of sons.
Galatians 4:3-5 KJV

At the exact predetermined time in history, God sent Jesus, the Seed of the woman, to free His chosen from the bonds of the law.

The incomprehensible worth of the blood of Christ

To summarize the doctrine of redemption, the focus will be on Christ as the Redeemer. Numerous passages will be referenced, beginning with the first book in the New Testament and ending with the last book in the Bible.

Jesus had revealed that the purpose of His first coming was to give His life as a ransom, i.e. to redeem His people from bondage to the world.

After Jesus' death, resurrection, and ascension, Paul addressed the leaders of the church at Ephesus. He admonished them to be true shepherds of the church which He described thusly:

...to feed the church of God, which he hath purchased with his own blood. Acts 20:28 KJV

With these words Paul acknowledged Christ as God and confirmed that believers in the current age, called the church, were purchased (ransomed) with His own blood.

Subsequently, Paul addressed the Christians in Rome where He emphasized that both Jews and gentiles were in bondage, and the remedy for both was the same.

For all have sinned, and come short of the glory of God, being justified freely by his grace through the redemption that is in Christ Jesus, whom God hath set forth to be a propitiation through faith in his blood... Romans 3:23-25a KJV

Propitiation is the required payment for reconciliation to God. God's mercy provided the propitiatory reconciliation.

Subsequently in the same letter, Paul taught that inasmuch as the Holy Spirit dwells in the heart of believers, the believer's body is the temple of God and must be respected as such and evidenced by one's behavior.

For ye are bought with a price; therefore, glorify God in your body and in your spirit, which are God's.
1 Corinthians 6:20 KJV

This verse confirms that after one is redeemed, i.e. bought with a price, the body and spirit of the redeemed belong to God. Therefore, the redeemed can glorify God by actions and thoughts.

Redemption for the church was God's plan from the foundation of the world

In Paul's letter to the church at Ephesus, he confirmed that God had predestined the redemption of Israel and the church from before time. God's plan included that His chosen would be adopted as sons by His Son Jesus. The reason for His plan was simply that He wanted to do it, i.e. "according to the good pleasure of His will."

God knew full well that man would fail to live up to His requirements; therefore, His remedy was also known from the foundation of the world.

In whom we have redemption through his blood, the forgiveness of sins, according to the riches of his grace, in which he hath abounded toward us in all wisdom... Ephesians 1:7 KJV

The immutable remedy includes blood and grace.

In his letter to the church at Colosse, Paul reiterates the deity of Christ and the gifts of deliverance and redemption.

"He has delivered us from the power of darkness and conveyed us into the kingdom of the Son of His love, in whom we have redemption through His blood, the forgiveness of sins. He is the image of the invisible God, the first born (preeminent) over all creation." Colossians 1:13-15 NKJV

'Delivered' describes the freedom from bondage which was accomplished by Christ who redeemed us by paying the required ransom. Christ is God and the Creator of all things, visible and invisible.

While mentoring and teaching Titus, Paul stressed God's grace exhibited through His Son Jesus. He admonished Titus to live and teach ways to glorify God.

"For the grace of God that brings salvation has appeared to all men, teaching us...that we should live soberly, righteously, and godly in the present age looking for the blessed hope and glorious appearing of our great God and Savior Jesus Christ, who gave Himself for us, that He might redeem us from every lawless deed..." Titus 2:11-14 NKJV

Paul's message was always consistent because truth doesn't change.

It is stressed that the mission of the Son at His first advent was to redeem His brethren from the curse of the law. Christ accomplished redemption by paying the debt He did not owe.

Thus His people are to acknowledge God's gift of grace by living godly during the present age while the Son is back with His Father in anticipation of His glorious return.

The writer of the book of Hebrews describes splendidly the purpose of Christ in terms of fulfilling the Old Covenant.

But Christ being come an high priest...neither by the blood of goats and calves, but by his own blood he entered in once into the holy place, having obtained eternal redemption for us. Hebrews 9:11-12 KJV

It had been said that it was impossible to forgive sins with the blood of animals which were offered many times, but Christ offered His blood once to obtain eternal redemption for His chosen.

God throughout the ages has revealed Himself and His standard of righteousness in great detail and in sequential steps to explain His purpose and plan. Man is without excuse.

Peter put it all together in plain words.

Forasmuch as ye know that ye were not redeemed with corruptible things, like silver and gold...but with the precious blood of Christ, as of a lamb without blemish and without spot, who verily was foreordained before the foundation of the world, but was manifest in these last times for you, who by him do believe in God... 1 Peter 1:18-21 KJV

Redemption of the soul could not be done with things subject to decay such as silver or gold, or in fact 'goats and calves.' The only payment for redemption was the shed blood of the Son of God. Christ's purpose had been since the foundation of the world but remained a mystery until the age of the church. And finally, to believe in God is also a gift of God.

The final passage takes place at the beginning of Daniel's 70th week. It describes the only one worthy to reclaim that which was lost in the curse.

...Thou art worthy to take the scroll, and to open its seals; for thou wast slain, and hast redeemed us to God by thy blood... Revelation 5:9 KJV

Praise God for His unfathomable gift of redemption!

Chapter 4

Abraham's 'Seed' in the Current Age

To properly comprehend the title material, it is necessary to examine the Old Testament foundation. It is extremely relevant in today's age to understand the history of Abraham's 'seed' leading up to the church age.

In fact, it is necessary to go back in the Bible approximately two millennia before Abraham.

And I will put enmity between thee and the woman, and between thy seed and her Seed... Genesis 3:15a KJV

God cursed the devil because of his deceit and told him from that time forward there would be enmity (hostility) between him and the woman, which God would 'put' (appoint) there. The enmity would extend for millennia through the seed, or offspring, of both the devil and the woman.

...he (seed of the woman) shall bruise thy head, and thou shalt bruise his heel. Genesis 3:15b KJV

God also revealed the ultimate victor, i.e. the Seed of the woman would bruise (break) the devil's head, while the devil and his seed would only be allowed to bruise the heel of the Seed of the woman.

God calls his servant from beyond the river

Now let's fast forward to the time of Abram.

While Abram and his family lived east of the Euphrates River where pagan gods were worshipped, God spoke to him and gave him specific commands.

...get thee out of thy country, and from thy kindred, and from thy father's house, unto a land that I will show thee; and I will make of thee a great nation, and I will bless thee, and make thy name great...And I will bless them that bless thee, and curse him that curseth thee: and in thee shall all families of the earth be blessed. Genesis 12:1-3 KJV

Notice how many 'I wills' are included in these verses. And notice particularly that God promised Abram that all the families of the earth would be blessed through him.

Another significant aspect of the above verses is that there are no conditions listed. There are no 'ifs.'

How did Abram respond to God's command to leave everything?

So Abram departed, as the LORD had spoken unto him...
Genesis 12:4 KJV

God alone ratified His covenant with Abram

The unconditional promises would be confirmed shortly thereafter when God ratified His covenant with Abram. The covenant with Abram would be ratified by God alone, while God caused a deep sleep to fall upon Abram.

As Abram and his wife were in the new land, they were childless. So Abram suggested to God that his servant Eliezer be counted as a descendant.

And, behold, the word of the LORD came unto him, saying, This shall not be thine heir; but he that shall come forth out of thine own loins shall be thine heir. Genesis 15:4 KJV

But Abram and Sarai were beyond childbearing years

Years passed and Abram and his wife were still childless, so Abram's wife Sarai suggested that Abram have a child with her handmaid Hagar. Sarai reasoned that such a child would indeed be Abram's son.

Hagar did conceive by Abram, and while carrying his child the Angel of the LORD spoke to her, and described the son she was about to bear.

...Behold, thou art with child, and shalt bear a son, and shalt call his name Ishmael...And he will be a wild man; his hand will be against every man and every man's hand against him; and he shall dwell in the presence of all his brethren. Genesis 16:11-12 KJV

The son fathered by Abram would be named Ishmael, and he would be an agitator. In addition he would be hated by all others.

The phrase 'wild man' in the above Scripture means wild donkey. The same Hebrew word is found later in the book of Job.

While Job was being interrogated by God, he was asked several questions including:

"Who set the wild donkey free? Who loosed the bonds of the onager (wild donkey), whose home I have made the wilderness, and the barren land his dwelling? He scorns the tumult of the city; he does not heed the shouts of the driver." Job 39:4-7 NKJV

God was telling Job that He formed the wild donkey and gave him his characteristics. God is also revealing that He fashioned Ishmael for His own purposes. Remember, 'I will put enmity...'

God changed the names of both Abram and Sarai

Abram became Abraham; from 'high father' to 'father of multitudes,' while Sarai became Sarah; from 'domineering' to 'princess.'

God said:

"No longer shall your name be called Abram, but your name shall be Abraham, for I have made you a father of many nations." Genesis 17:5 NKJV

Then God changed Sarai's name.

"As for Sarai your wife, you shall not call her name Sarai, but Sarah shall be her name. And I will bless her and also give you a son by her...and she shall be a mother of nations; kings of peoples shall be from her." Genesis 17:15-16 NKJV

At this point Abraham was very skeptical because he would be 100 years old when Sarah would have a child, and Sarah would be 90 years old.

Seeing that his son by Hagar was already 10 years old, Abraham offered Ishmael as the heir to the covenant.

God was patient with Abraham again as he renounced his suggestion.

And God said, Sarah, thy wife, shall bear thee a son indeed; and thou shalt call his name Isaac; and I will

establish my covenant with him for an everlasting covenant, and with his seed after him. Genesis 17:19 KJV

God then did something profound for Abraham's son Ishmael which would have long term effects.

"And as for Ishmael, I have heard you. Behold, I have blessed him, and will make him fruitful, and will multiply him exceedingly. He shall beget twelve princes, and I will make him a great nation." Genesis 17:20 NKJV

Ishmael did father twelve sons who became the tribes of Arabia.

Then God fulfilled His promise to Abraham and Sarah.

"And the LORD visited Sarah as He had said, and the LORD did for Sarah as He had spoken. For Sarah conceived and bore Abraham a son in his old age, at the set time of which God had spoken to him." Genesis 21:1-2 NKJV

Enmity begins with Sarah and Hagar

A great deal of enmity ensued between Sarah and Hagar, as well as between their sons Isaac and Ishmael.

When Isaac was approximately three years old and Ishmael was in his teen years, Abraham honored Isaac's weaning with a great feast.

And the child grew, and was weaned: and Abraham made a great feast the same day that Isaac was weaned. Genesis 21:8 KJV

At that weaning celebration, something happened that would affect the two sons for millennia.

And Sarah saw the son of Hagar...whom she had borne unto Abraham, mocking. Wherefore she said unto Abraham, Cast out this bondwoman and her son; for the son of this bondwoman shall not be heir with my son, even with Isaac. Genesis 21:9-10 KJV

Such animosity would prevail through the ages.

Hagar was the bond woman, and her son Ishmael was the son born according to the flesh.

Sarah was the free woman, and her son Isaac was the son born according to God's promise.

That would, from that time forward, define the two sides of the enmity between the seed of the devil and the Seed of the woman.

The sons of promise would accept God's gracious gift of salvation by faith, while the sons born according to the flesh would attempt to earn salvation through performance.

Ishmael and others from the 'east' would attempt to destroy Isaac (Israel) from the face of the earth

In our previous book entitled: ***Looking Backward from the Future*** many of those of the 'east' were identified and described including:

- The sons of Ishmael

- The sons of Abraham through Keturah

- Job's advisors

The psalmist revealed such a plot to destroy Israel by their enemies.

"For behold, Your enemies make a tumult (uproar); and those who hate You have lifted up their head. They have taken crafty counsel against Your people..." Psalm 83:2-3 NKJV

Then the specific objective of the 'coalition of destruction' was revealed.

"They have said, 'Come and let us cut them off from being a nation, that the name of Israel may be remembered no more.' For they have consulted together with one consent; they form a confederacy against You..." Psalm 83:4-5 NKJV

And then the conspirators are named.

"The tents of Edom and the Ishmaelites; Moab and the Hagrites..." Psalm 83:6 NKJV

Edom is Esau, while Moab descended from Lot. Then there is Ishmael, and those named after his mother Hagar.

God's response to such a conspiracy?

"Why do the nations rage, and the people plot a vain thing? The kings of the earth set themselves, and the rulers take counsel together, against the LORD and against His Anointed, saying, 'Let us break Their bonds in pieces and cast away Their cords from us.'" Psalm 2:1-3 NKJV

God's Anointed is Jesus Christ, the ultimate Seed of the woman through Abraham and Isaac. The plot to destroy Israel (named after Isaac's son Jacob) is utter foolishness.

He who sitteth in the heavens shall laugh; the Lord shall have them in derision. Psalm 2:4 KJV

Both 'laugh' and 'derision' mean to 'mock,' to 'scorn,' to 'make sport.'

Ishmael and those of the east have desired to destroy Israel from being a nation from ages past; and nothing has changed today.

Now recall what Ishmael did to Isaac at Isaac's weaning celebration.

And Sarah saw the son of Hagar...whom she had borne unto Abraham, mocking (scoffing). Genesis 21:9 KJV

'Scoffing' means to 'mock,' to 'scorn,' to 'make sport.'

Ishmael scoffed at Isaac when Ishmael was in his teen years.

The Seed of the woman

Approximately two millennia after the time of Abraham, the birth of the ultimate Seed of the woman was announced by Gabriel.

"And behold, you will conceive in your womb, and bear a son, and you shall name Him Jesus. He will be great, and will be called the Son of the Most High; and the Lord God will give Him the throne of His father David; and He will reign over the house of Jacob forever; and His kingdom will have no end." Luke 1:31-33 NASB

The family tree of the Seed of the woman is found in the first chapter of the gospel records.

The book of the genealogy of Jesus Christ, the son of David, the son of Abraham. To Abraham was born Isaac; and to Isaac, Jacob; and to Jacob, Judah and his brothers... Matthew 1:1-2 NASB

Jesus placed Ishmael in perspective for the current age

Recall, the major difference between Ishmael and his seed, and Isaac and his seed, is that Ishmael was the son born according to the flesh inasmuch as he was the son of the bondwoman, Hagar.

Isaac was the son born of promise, the son of the free woman Sarah, the wife of Abraham.

Both Ishmael and Isaac were sons of Abraham; however, God's immutable covenant with Abraham would be perpetuated through Isaac, and not Ishmael.

Therefore spiritually, being of the lineage of Abraham was not an advantage for Ishmael. The Pharisees subsequently adopted the thinking of Ishmael, relying on their physical heritage to Abraham as their security.

During Jesus' time on earth He continually called out the Pharisees, inasmuch as they exhibited the characteristics of Ishmael.

For example the Pharisees were intent on trying to obey the law to gain God's favor, while dismissing Jesus' message of grace.

The Pharisees continued pressing their argument that their security was based on Abraham's being their father.

They answered Him, "We are Abraham's offspring, and have never yet been enslaved to anyone; how is it that You say, 'You shall become free?'" John 8:33 NASB

Jesus' response:

"I know that you are Abraham's offspring; yet you seek to kill Me, because My word has no place in you. I speak

the things which I have seen with My Father; therefore you also do the things which you heard from your father."
John 8:37-38 NASB

"Truly, truly, I say to you, before Abraham was born, I AM." Therefore they picked up stones to throw at Him...
John 8:58-59 NASB

Then Jesus highlighted the hypocrisy of those born of the flesh.

"But woe to you, scribes and Pharisees, hypocrites, because you shut off the kingdom of heaven from men; for you do not enter in yourselves, nor do you allow those who are entering to go in...you travel about on sea and land to make one proselyte; and when he becomes one, you make him twice as much a son of hell as yourselves."
Matthew 23:13, 15 NASB

And finally, Jesus described in detail who the father is of those born of the flesh.

"You are of your father the devil, and you want to do the desires of your father. He was a murderer from the beginning, and does not stand in the truth, because there is no truth in him. Whenever he speaks a lie, he speaks from his own nature; for he is a liar, and the father of lies."
John 8:44 NASB

Thus, Jesus proclaimed that the Pharisees and their doctrine were of the devil.

The Pharisees rejected Jesus' claim to deity

On a particular Sabbath day, Jesus not only healed a sick man, but also claimed that God was His Father.

For this cause therefore the Jews were seeking all the more to kill Him, because He not only was breaking the Sabbath, but also was calling God His own Father, Making Himself equal with God. John 5:18 NASB

The unbelieving Jews continued to push Jesus to prove that He was the Son of God.

Jesus answered them, "I told you, and you do not believe; the works that I do in My Father's name, these bear witness of Me. But you do not believe, because you are not of My sheep...I and the Father are one."
John 10:25-26, 30 NASB

Jesus explained to them that they did not belong to Him, and then He equated Himself to His Father.

The enmity not only continued; it accelerated.

Isaac's weaning feast would have profound effects on the church

As the sons grew older the scoffing and mocking became more serious, as revealed by Paul.

"Now we, brethren, as Isaac was, are children of promise. But, as he who was born according to the flesh then persecuted him who was born according to the Spirit, even so it is now." Galatians 4:29 NKJV

Paul described the animosity toward the son of the free woman by Ishmael as persecution. Persecution in this context is from the Greek *dioko* meaning 'to pursue with repeated acts of enmity.'

This relationship can be traced back to the early days in the garden as noted at the beginning of this chapter.

And I will put enmity between thee and the woman, and between thy seed and her seed; he shall bruise thy head, and thou shalt bruise his heel. Genesis 3:15 KJV

Paul explains the relativity of Ishmael and Isaac to the church

Recall, Ishmael was the result of personal efforts by Sarah and Abraham to fulfill God's plan and was thus called the son born according to the flesh.

Isaac, on the other hand, was the result exclusively of God alone fulfilling His promise that Abraham and Sarah, who were both far beyond childbearing age, would have a son together. Therefore, Isaac is called the son of promise.

Then Paul put it in perspective.

"Tell me, you who want to be under law, do you not listen to the law? For it is written that Abraham had two sons, one by the bondwoman and one by the free woman. But the son by the bondwoman was born according to the flesh, and the son by the free woman through the promise." Galatians 4:21-23 NASB

Just as Ishmael scoffed at Isaac when Isaac was just a small child, Paul revealed that the son born according to the flesh was, 2,000 years later, persecuting the church, founded by the son of promise.

In other words, all who attempt to attain salvation by personal effort are persecuting the church, which embraces that salvation is exclusively a gracious gift of God promised to the believer and accepted by faith.

Paul then instructs the church on how to handle the ideology of salvation by personal effort.

But what does the Scripture say? "CAST OUT THE BONDWOMAN AND HER SON, FOR THE SON OF THE BONDWOMAN SHALL NOT BE AN HEIR WITH THE SON OF THE FREE WOMAN." Galatians 4:30 NASB

These were the same words spoken by Isaac's mother Sarah after she witnessed Ishmael deriding her son.

Paul confirms that the son born according to the flesh was not Abraham's spiritual seed

Recall, many of those who persecuted Jesus thought they had found favor with God, inasmuch as they were Abraham's physical descendants.

Paul addressed that issue succinctly.

...For they are not all Israel who are descended from Israel; neither are they all children because they are Abraham's descendants, but: "THROUGH ISAAC YOUR DESCENDANTS WILL BE NAMED." That is, it is not the children of the flesh who are children of God, but the children of the promise are regarded as descendants. For this is a word of promise: "AT THIS TIME I WILL COME AND SARAH SHALL HAVE A SON." Romans 9:6b-9 NASB

Perhaps the most contentious discussions Jesus had with the Pharisees focused on the confidence they placed on their heritage.

And then there are those, in fact the majority of all mankind, who place their security in doing good works, i.e. attempting to obey God's law through personal effort.

"...knowing that a man is not justified (declared righteous) by the works of the law but by faith in...Christ and not by the works of the law; for by the works of the law no flesh shall be justified." Galatians 2:16 NKJV

While the true sons of Abraham are being preserved during this present age, the seeds of Ishmael are relentlessly persecuting them and will continue to do so until the end of the tribulation.

Paul warned the church, i.e. all the sons of promise through Abraham, to be on guard against false and deceitful teaching.

"See to it that no one takes you captive through, philosophy and empty deception, according to the tradition of men, according to the elementary principles of the world, rather than according to Christ. For in Him all the fullness of Deity dwells in bodily form, and in Him you have been made complete, and He is the head over all rule and authority." Colossians 2:8-10 NASB

Paul concludes the argument.

So then, brethren, we are not children of a bondwoman, but of the free woman. It was for freedom that Christ set us free; therefore keep standing firm and do not be subject again to a yoke of slavery." Galatians 4:31-5:1 NASB

Christ is everything!

Abraham simply took God at His word

What then shall we say that Abraham, our forefather according to the flesh, has found? For if Abraham was justified by works, he has something to boast about; but

not before God. For what does the Scripture say? "AND ABRAHAM BELIEVED GOD, AND IT WAS RECKONED TO HIM AS RIGHTEOUSNESS." Romans 4:1-3 NASB

All who take God at His word can claim Abraham as their father. Just as Abraham believed God for that which he couldn't see, the sons of promise must do likewise.

"...but also to those who are of the faith of Abraham, who is the father of us all (as it is written, 'I have made you a father of many nations')...he did not waver at the promise of God through unbelief, but was strengthened in faith... fully convinced that what He had promised He was also able to perform." Romans 4:16, 20-21 NKJV

Abraham brushed all earthly limitations aside and simply took God at His word. Christians share Abraham's faith and trust.

"Now it was not written for his (Abraham's) sake alone... but also for us...who believe..." Romans 4:23-24 NKJV

And though God's promises to Abraham originally focused on the future nation of Israel, all those with the faith of Abraham would be blessed throughout the ages.

Therefore, be sure that it is those who are of faith that are sons of Abraham, and the Scripture, foreseeing that God would justify the Gentiles by faith, preached the gospel beforehand to Abraham, saying, "ALL THE NATIONS

SHALL BE BLESSED IN YOU." So then those who are of faith are blessed with Abraham, the believer.
Galatians 3:7-9 NASB

Therefore, Christians, i.e. the true church, are Abraham's spiritual seed.

And if ye be Christ's, then are ye Abraham's seed, and heirs according to the promise. Galatians 3:29 KJV

And lastly, the writer of Hebrews provided a glimpse of what Abraham believed about the future. Note again the seeds of promise, i.e. Isaac and Jacob.

By faith Abraham, when he was called, obeyed by going out to a place which he was to receive for an inheritance; and he went out, not knowing where he was going. By faith he lived as an alien in the land of promise, as in a foreign land, dwelling in tents with Isaac and Jacob, fellow-heirs of the same promise; for he was looking for the city which has foundations, whose architect and builder is God.
Hebrews 11:8-10 NASB

Abraham was totally confident that some day he would see the glorious New Jerusalem, the heavenly city not built with hands. Abraham was so confident in God's word, that he left everything he had and journeyed to a foreign land, not knowing where he was going, or what he would be doing when he arrived there.

Do not add to the word of God, or offer any private interpretation

The Bible is consistently clear about adding to the word of God as written.

"You shall not add to the word which I am commanding you, nor take away from it, that you may keep the commandments of the LORD your God which I command you." Deuteronomy 4:2 NASB

The Bible reiterated that same truth approximately 500 years later.

"Every word of God is pure...Do not add to His words, lest He rebuke you, and you be found a liar." Proverbs 30:5-6 NKJV

And then the final words in the Bible stress that same warning.

I testify to everyone who hears the words of the prophecy of this book: if anyone adds to them, God shall add to him the plagues which are written in this book; and if anyone takes away from the words of the book of this prophecy, God shall take away his part from the tree of life and from the holy city... Revelation 22:18-19 NASB

A tale of two donkeys

To summarize this chapter, recall the description of Ishmael provided to Hagar by the Angel of the LORD before he was born.

- He shall be a wild man (onager, wild donkey).

- His hand shall be against every man.

- Every man's hand shall be against him.

God revealed more characteristics of the wild donkey to Job.

- He scorns the tumult of the city.

- He does not heed the shouts of the driver.

Therefore, the Bible describes Ishmael as a wild man who will take orders from no one and is at odds with all those around him.

Judah's donkey

Now let's turn to Jacob's blessings to his sons prior to his death in Egypt in 1858 BC. Of particular interest is Jacob's blessing to his son Judah. Most remember that blessing as it applied to Judah being a lion and a king.

But consider the latter part of the blessing.

"Binding his foal unto the vine, and his (donkey's) colt unto the choice vine, he washed his garments in wine, and his clothes in the blood of grapes" Genesis 49:11 KJV

'Foal' does in fact mean 'colt' or 'young.' Thus the offspring is the subject. Judah would tie the colt to the choice vine of the vineyard.

However, the Hebrew for 'colt' in the above verse is *Ben* which means a young male child. It is the same word used to describe the two 'children' within Rebekah, i.e. Jacob and Esau.

Further consider the following:

"For unto us a child is born, unto us a son is given, and the government shall be upon his shoulder..."
Isaiah 9:6a KJV

'Son' in the above is also from the Hebrew *Ben*, while 'child' is synonymous with 'Son.' Isaiah further describes the Son as a Prince which is a masculine noun. In the referenced verse the pronoun 'his' is used to describe the future reign of the 'Son.'

Note also from Genesis 49:11 that the colt *(Ben)* will be tied to the 'choice vine.'

Isaiah described the nation of Israel as a vineyard planted by God.

*"And he dug (fenced) it, and gathered out the stones, and planted it with the **choicest vine**, and built a tower in the midst of it, and also made a winepress in it; and he looked for it to bring forth grapes, and it brought forth wild grapes."* Isaiah 5:2 KJV (emphasis mine)

Therefore, Judah tied the 'colt' to the 'choicest vine,' which is the same term Isaiah used to describe God's vineyard.

The meaning of the vineyard is confirmed.

"For the vineyard of the LORD of hosts is the house of Israel..." Isaiah 5:7a KJV

From wine to blood

"...he washed his garments in wine, and his clothes in the blood of grapes." Genesis 49:11b KJV

'Washed' has several meanings including 'trample' or 'tread.'

In Hebrew, garments and clothes are synonymous. 'Wine' in this verse is used interchangeably with 'banqueting,' while 'blood' means 'slaughter' and is also used to describe the juice of grapes.

Now consider the following written over 1,300 years after Jacob's words to his son Judah, and 500 years before the prophecy was fulfilled.

"Rejoice greatly, O daughter of Zion; shout, O daughter of Jerusalem; behold, thy King cometh unto thee; he is just, and having salvation; lowly, and riding upon a (donkey), and upon a colt, the foal of a (donkey)." Zechariah 9:9 KJV

'Foal' in this passage is likewise from the Hebrew *'Ben'* meaning a young male child. It appears that the foal is a male offspring of Judah, carrying the King.

Zechariah's prophecy was perfectly fulfilled when Jesus rode into Jerusalem at the beginning of the last week of His life before the cross.

Connecting the dots

Thus, while Ishmael was/is a wild, uncontrollable, donkey; Jesus presented Himself as Messiah riding on the colt of a donkey. The colt was obviously domesticated and subservient to his rider.

The colt was metaphorically attached to the nation of Israel.

So Jesus during His initial time on earth was lowly, riding on the foal of a tamed donkey; however, He will exchange the colt for a majestic white horse when He returns to end the great tribulation.

The world will see Jesus' clothes covered with blood just as was Judah's clothes as described by his father Jacob.

"And I saw heaven opened and, behold, a white horse; and he that sat upon him was called Faithful and True..." Revelation 19:11a KJV

"And he was clothed with a vesture dipped in blood; and his name is called The Word of God." Revelation 19:13 KJV

"And out of his mouth goeth a sharp sword, that with it he should smite the nations, and he shall rule them with a rod of iron; and he treadeth the winepress of the fierceness and wrath of Almighty God." Revelation 19:15 KJV

The battle of the brothers, which began in the garden, comes to an end!

Chapter 5

Suppressing the Truth in the Current Age

The majority of mankind will not spend eternity with their Creator. The majority will have been deceived into believing the lie concerning the reality of Christ. Christ is God in the flesh, Redeemer of mankind, and the only way to know God the Father. Any other representation of the person and mission of Christ is false, and anyone who embraces any lesser role of Christ has been deceived.

Therefore, the focus of the Bible is to present Christ as the only way to attain God's required standard of righteousness. The Bible is also very clear to describe and define the works of the enemy; the father of lies and master deceiver.

Adam and Eve were created in the image of God. In fact, they were the only created beings made in God's image. In the Garden of Eden they had everything, including the appointed privilege of having dominion over all other living creatures on the earth.

Distorting the truth

But God's arch enemy, who had fallen from grace due to his pride, had in his heart the goal to interfere in God's plan for Adam and Eve by deception.

"Now the serpent was more cunning than any beast of the field which the LORD God had made." Genesis 3:1 NKJV

Different translations use different words to describe the serpent's stratagem and purpose. For example, the NKJV uses 'cunning' while other translations use 'subtle,' 'crafty,' and 'shrewd,' along with several other synonymous descriptive words.

We all know the story. Eve was enticed to partake of the fruit of the tree of the knowledge of good and evil, which God had specifically forbidden.

Her response when questioned about her disobedience:

"The serpent deceived me, and I ate." Genesis 3:13b NASB

That was the beginning of the great deception. The word 'deceived' also has many synonyms including 'ensnare,' 'beguile,' 'entrap,' 'entice,' 'lie,' 'delude,' and 'mislead.'

The sin of deception that began in the Garden of Eden will prevail, and in fact accelerate, until the great deceiver is ultimately defeated and cast into the everlasting lake of fire.

Thus, deception is present from the early chapters of Genesis through the final chapters of Revelation.

And when the thousand years are completed, Satan will be released from his prison, and will come out to deceive the nations...and fire came down from heaven and devoured them. And the devil who deceived them was thrown into the lake of fire and brimstone, where the beast and the false prophet are also; and they will be tormented day and night forever and ever. Revelation 20:7-10 NASB

Let's review how deception has affected God's people throughout history.

Deadly affects of embracing deceit

After Adam and Eve's initial sin in the garden, all mankind was born without the Spirit of God. Recall, God had breathed 'life' into Adam.

Therefore, all mankind was subsequently born innately evil. Such prevails even to this day. A person must be 'born again' to receive the Spirit of God to overcome his evil nature.

"The heart is more deceitful than all else and is desperately sick..." Jeremiah 17:9 NASB

The wisest man in the world, Solomon, addressed the issue also.

...Furthermore, the hearts of the sons of men are full of evil, and insanity is in their hearts throughout their lives... Ecclesiastes 9:3 NASB

Solomon's wisdom was similar to the wisdom expressed by Jeremiah the prophet. Both proclaimed that unredeemed mankind is inherently evil by nature. And it must be kept in mind that God's chosen who receive wisdom to overpower ungodly natural tendencies, such as deceit and evil, are in the distinct minority.

Pride is also a cause of much deceit. For example, any nation that depends on their own strength for survival or victory has been deceived. God will personally bring them down in humility in His timing. Consider Edom's judgment.

"The pride of your heart has deceived you...You who say in your heart, 'Who will bring me down to the ground?' 'Though you ascend as high as the eagle...from there I will bring you down,' says the LORD." Obadiah 1:3 NKJV

The challenge of innate deceit was, is, and will be very active through the ages, especially in the present age of the church.

The arrival of Jesus caused great division

Jesus confirmed the great division that would be present during His first advent on earth, even within families. Such division is between the called versus those who are not.

"Do you suppose that I came to grant peace on earth? I tell you, no, but rather division; for from now on five members in one household will be divided, three against two, and two against three. They will be divided, father against son, and son against father..." Luke 12:51-53a NASB

The division will be between those who commit to the gospel message, versus those who reject the gospel.

When Jesus began to teach the crowds, there was great division; some believed His words while others did not.

For example, on the last day of the Feast of Tabernacles, a pitcher of water from the pool of Siloam was poured out as a sacrifice on the altar. On one such feast Jesus cried out:

"...If any man is thirsty, let him come to Me and drink. He who believes in Me, as the Scripture said, 'From his innermost being shall flow rivers of living water.'"
John 37b-38 NASB

He was, of course, speaking of the Holy Spirit that would enter into the hearts of those who would believe in Him. However, this teaching caused great controversy.

So there arose a division in the multitude because of Him. John 7:43 NASB

Recall also the controversy over Jesus healing the blind man on the Sabbath day. The man had been blind since birth.

The miracle was witnessed by many; however, some who witnessed the healing still wouldn't accept Jesus' authority.

Therefore some of the Pharisees were saying, "This man is not from God, because He does not keep the Sabbath." But others were saying, "How can a man who is a sinner perform such signs?" And there was a division among them. John 9:16 NASB

Jesus continued to teach that He was the Son of God, inasmuch as He had the power to lay down His life and be raised up from the grave. Some said He had a demon, while others believed, remembering His previous miracles.

*There arose a division again among the Jews because of these words.*John 10:19 NASB

Subsequently Paul warned of division during the church age, and even within the church

And then during the church age, there was great division between the believers and the deniers. Consider the contention caused by Paul and Barnabas when they preached the gospel message to both Jews and Greeks.

But the Jews who disbelieved stirred up the minds of the Gentiles, and embittered them against the brethren...but the multitude of the city was divided; and some sided with the Jews, and some with the apostles. Acts 14:2, 4 NASB

Again, the division was caused by preaching and teaching the gospel message of Jesus Christ.

Now I urge you, brethren, keep your eye on those who cause dissensions and hindrances contrary to the teaching which you learned, and turn away from them. For such men are slaves not of our Lord Christ but of their own appetites; and by their smooth and flattering speech they deceive the hearts of the unsuspecting. Romans 16:17-18 NASB

There was even division in the church at Corinth concerning the Lord's Supper. The commemoration became more of a gluttonous feast than a remembrance of the Lord fulfilling the Old Covenant and instituting the New.

For, in the first place, when you come together as a church, I hear that divisions exist among you...
1 Corinthians 11:18 NASB

Not much has changed.

Deception begins with a lie

Inasmuch as Satan is the father of lies, and rules the world in this present age, it could be expected that he is very busy during this gap between Daniel's 69th and 70th week, i.e. the age of the church. And so it is.

The primary Greek word used in this section will be *pseudos* or its derivatives, which means basically 'to lie' or 'tell a falsehood.' Therefore the passages referenced will contain the English words 'lie' or 'false.'

A liar in the present context is one who deceives others by tempting them into idolatry, or spiritual adultery, by rejecting the truth.

"For out of the heart come evil thoughts...false witness... slanders. These are the things which defile the man..." Matthew 15:19 NASB

Jesus was reiterating that to bear false witness was in the heart of a natural man, i.e. it was a natural thing to do. Such could only be overcome by the power and presence of the Spirit.

In the early church there were those who were more concerned about personal gain than spreading the gospel.

For such men are false apostles, deceitful workers, disguising themselves as apostles of Christ. And no wonder, for even Satan disguises himself as an angel of light. 2 Corinthians 11:13-14 NASB

Jesus warned of deception

The disciple Mark records a parable of Jesus thusly:

"...there is nothing outside the man which going into him can defile him; but the things which proceed out of the man are what defile the man."

Mark 7:15 NASB

When asked to expound on the parable Jesus responded:

"For from within, out of the heart of men, proceed the evil thoughts...wickedness, as well as deceit...pride...all these evil things proceed from within and defile the man." Mark 7:21-23 NASB

So Jesus confirmed the Old Testament truth that men are born with such ungodly traits as deceit and pride. The Old Testament also proclaimed that 'the LORD abhors the bloodthirsty and deceitful man.'

Just prior to His crucifixion, Jesus gave His disciples explicit warnings of events that would happen during the church age preceding His return to end the great tribulation. He specifically warned to be on the alert for those who would attempt to deceive His chosen.

*"Then many false prophets will rise up and deceive many..."*Matthew 24:11 NKJV

The Greek for 'deceive' is similar to the Hebrew. It means 'to be led astray,' 'to be seduced,' 'ensnared,' 'lured,' 'to err from the truth.'

"For false christs and false prophets will rise and show great signs and wonders to deceive (mislead), if possible, even the elect. See, I have told you beforehand." Matthew 24:24-25 NKJV

The apostles continued to warn the church of deception within

After Jesus' death, resurrection, and ascension, His apostles gave many examples of such deceit in the churches and warned them to be on guard.

Paul was an ardent teacher to warn of such trickery. He taught and preached that a great defense against deception was for one to grow in the word.

...we are no longer to be children, tossed here and there by waves, and carried about by every wind of doctrine, by the trickery of men, by craftiness in deceitful scheming... Ephesians 4:14 NASB

Notice Paul employed timeless terms which described the enemy's methodology in the Garden of Eden, i.e. 'trickery,' 'craftiness,' and 'deceitful.' Nothing has changed.

Paul then told of the condemnation of those who deceived God's chosen.

"Let no one deceive you with empty words, for because of these things the wrath of God comes upon the sons of disobedience." Ephesians 5:6 NASB

In his letter to the church at Colosse, Paul warned them again to beware of the teachings of men who spoke from within their natural selves, lacking the wisdom of Christ.

See to it that no one take you captive through philosophy and empty deception, according to the tradition of men, according to the elementary principles of the world, rather than according to Christ. Colossians 2:8 NASB

Deceit includes teaching philosophy in place of Scripture and that which appeals to the 'world' and not the kingdom. The 'tradition of men' appeals to the natural man and includes present rewards vs. the promise of eternal rewards.

It is quite easy to identify contemporary church teaching; that which appeals to itching ears. Such churches are experiencing tremendous growth while deceiving many.

Itching ears receive and embrace untruth

Peter also said much about false prophets in the past and also false teachers during the present age. He spoke of their methodology and their fate.

"But there were also false prophets among the people, even as there will be false teachers among you, who will secretly bring in destructive heresies...and many will follow their destructive ways, because of whom the way of truth will be blasphemed. By covetousness they will exploit you with deceptive words..." 2 Peter 2:1-3a NKJV

Key points include there will be false teachers in the church and the truth will be blasphemed. Deceptive words would include such promises as health and prosperity in the present age. Such teaching is rampant in many churches today.

Christ had a good word for the church in Ephesus in His message to the churches in the final book of the Bible.

"I know your works, your labor, your patience, and that you cannot bear those who are evil. And you have tested those who say they are apostles and are not, and have found them liars..." Revelation 2:2 NKJV

The church at Ephesus, with Spiritual discernment, tested the doctrine of those claiming to be apostles of God. The church must not give credence to such, but be prepared to deal with them.

Everyone has the choice of accepting the truth or the lie. Either choice is forever.

John's epistles confirmed that deceit began with the devil

The apostle John had much to say about deceit: its source and its presence.

Little children, let no one deceive you; the one who practices righteousness is righteous, just as He is righteous; the one who practices sin is of the devil; for the devil has sinned from the beginning. The Son of God appeared for this purpose, that He might destroy the works of the devil. 1 John 3:7-8 NASB

John confirmed that the redeemed have been made righteous just as their Redeemer. He also confirmed that the devil, i.e. the great deceiver was in the Garden to deceive those first created in the image of God, although the devil's first sin of pride occurred long before God created man.

The truth that Christ would destroy the devil was also revealed in the Garden. Recall the devil's fate resulting from the curse.

"...Because you have done this...I will put enmity between you and the woman, and between your seed and her seed; He shall bruise you on the head, and you shall bruise him on the heel." Genesis 3:14a, 15 NASB

A major point of this book is that Christ is the ultimate Seed of the woman.

Then John confirmed that the many deceivers in the present age are anti-Christs. The deceit is nearly always focused on the person and mission of Jesus Christ.

For many deceivers have gone out into the world, those who do not acknowledge Jesus Christ as coming in the flesh. This is the deceiver and the antichrist. 2 John 7 NASB

The challenge to the churches today is straightforward; teach and preach the truth of Christ, Christ, Christ!

Deceit is inevitable – recognize and confront it

Deceit runs rampant throughout the world and, as has been noted, will be found even at the end of the future millennial kingdom.

Also as previously noted, it all began in the Garden of Eden.

Eve's disobedience had universal effects. She was tricked into doing something that, while appealing to the senses, was directly contrary to her Creator's instructions.

And so it was that the war between good and evil had come to earth.

The writers of the New Testament related church age deceit to Eve's actions. Paul warned against falling for false doctrine.

But I am afraid, lest as the serpent deceived Eve by his craftiness, your minds should be led astray from the simplicity and purity of devotion to Christ. 2 Corinthians 11:3 NASB

The deception described by Paul is the false doctrine that salvation requires something more than the vicarious death of Christ. The early church had to deal extensively with such heresy.

Mankind is totally impotent to offer any assistance in the miracle of salvation. Man can only respond to the call after the Spirit of God initially stirs his heart.

Jesus warned in no uncertain terms that deceit would not only be present throughout the church age, but would, in fact, increase as week 70 approached.

Apostasy in the church is the fruit of deception

Jesus told the people that there would be those who couldn't accept the truth of who He really was.

Many therefore of His disciples, when they heard this said, "This is a difficult statement; who can listen to it?"... As a result of this many of His disciples withdrew, and were not walking with Him any more. John 6:60, 66 NASB

Then Jesus revealed that there would be many pretenders who were not true followers.

"Not every one who says to Me, 'Lord, Lord,' will enter the kingdom of heaven; but he who does the will of My Father who is in heaven." Matthew 7:21 NASB

Paul continued to warn the church against false teaching.

But the Spirit explicitly says that in later times some will fall away from the faith, paying attention to deceitful spirits and doctrines of demons, by means of the hypocrisy of liars... 1 Timothy 4:1-2 NASB

Those who depart were never true members of the kingdom to begin with. And Paul revealed that deceiving spirits and demons are one and the same.

The final great apostasy will pave the way for anti-Christ

In his second letter to the church at Thessalonica, Paul stressed the great apostasy that will be experienced during the climax of the church age.

Let no one in any way deceive you, for it will not come unless the apostasy comes first, and the man of lawlessness is revealed, the son of destruction... 2 Thessalonians 2:3 NASB

Paul was explaining that the church will be purged prior to the revelation of the anti-Christ.

And then Paul confirms that those who fall away were never part of the true church.

And then that lawless one will be revealed...with all the deception of wickedness for those who perish, because they did not receive the love of the truth so as to be saved. And for this reason God will send upon them a deluding influence so that they might believe what is false (the lie)... 2 Thessalonians 2:8a, 10-11 NASB

The church needs to be aware of such within their pews, and relentlessly preach the simplicity found in Christ.

The lawless one is a puppet of the devil himself along with his accomplice, the false prophet. Both will find their destiny in the lake of fire after attempting war with the returning Christ.

*And the beast was seized, and with him the false prophet...these two were thrown alive into the lake of fire which burns with brimstone.*Revelation 19:20 NASB

At that time the devil himself will be locked in the bottomless pit to be released after the millennium in an attempt to deceive the nations one last time.

Demonic activity during the church age

If deceit, lies, and division weren't enough, there is also much demonic activity during the present age.

Demons are spirits of fallen angels. While many are temporarily confined to the bottomless pit, many are very active in world affairs today serving their master the devil. In fact, demons are perhaps the major implementers of Satan's deceitful agenda.

And many of those imprisoned demons in the bottomless pit will be released during the rapidly approaching tribulation period to punish unrepentant mankind. We'll examine that aspect shortly.

Demonic activity isn't new. Such activity was noted in ancient Israel as well as spoken of in the New Testament including the final book of the Bible, i.e. the Revelation of Jesus Christ.

Let's go back several thousand years and review a profound passage from the Psalms that describes the range of Israel's sins.

And (they) served their (Gentile's) idols...They even sacrificed their sons and their daughters to the demons, and shed innocent blood, the blood of their sons and their daughters... Psalm 106:36-38a NASB

The Hebrew word for 'demons' is 'devils.' The Hebrew word for 'sacrificed' has several synonyms including 'slaughter' and 'kill.'

Newborn innocent children were slaughtered and offered to demons. Such was an abomination to God.

Demons influence the nonbeliever by impersonating idols made with hands. Therefore, any sacrifice offered by a nonbeliever is by definition offered to demons.

According to Paul:

...the things which the Gentiles sacrifice, they sacrifice to demons and not to God; and I do not want you to become sharers in demons. 1 Corinthians 10:20 NASB

Contemporary divisions

Consider the major divisions within our nation today. One of the most contentious issues is the definition of when life begins for a child. The Bible is very clear. Thus the divisions in America are in essence between those who live by Biblical teachings and those who do not.

How does this affect America's future?

Consider the words of Jesus.

"Any kingdom divided against itself is laid waste; and any city or house divided against itself shall not stand." Matthew 12:25 NASB

But the influence of demons goes far beyond sacrifices; it includes false and deceitful teaching.

As previously stated:

But the Spirit explicitly says that in later times some will fall away from the faith, paying attention to deceitful spirits and doctrines of demons, by means of the hypocrisy of liars... 1 Timothy 4:1-2a NASB

Submission to demonic influence will accelerate during this age and come to a head during the great tribulation. Regardless of the extent of tribulation hardship, the nonbeliever will cling to demonically inspired idols.

The sixth trumpet judgment during the great tribulation describes the refusal of nonbelievers to repudiate demonic influence.

Demons from the bottomless pit will be released to kill one-third of mankind, and yet those who survive will not repent from demon worship.

"But the rest of mankind, who were not killed by these plagues, did not repent of the works of their hands, that they should not worship demons, and idols of gold, silver, brass, stone, and wood, which can neither see nor hear nor walk." Revelation 9:20 NKJV

Recall that demons are the implementers of moral evil and they influence the nonbeliever to cling to false gods. The Greek word for 'demons' is also 'devils.'

Non-repentant mankind will continue to worship demons and place their trust in idols of gold, silver...

Then John lists several activities that will not be abandoned because of deceit, lies, division, or demonic activities.

...and they did not repent of their murders nor of their sorceries nor of their immorality nor of their thefts. Revelation 9:21 NASB

Murder *(phonos)* means 'slaughter,' 'butcher,' 'cut to pieces.'

Sorcery *(pharmakeia)* means 'drugs,' 'occult' or 'magical incantation with drugs.'

Sexual immorality *(porneia)* includes any kind of sexual sin.

Thefts *(klepto)* means not only 'to steal,' but has the additional meanings 'to seize,' or 'take by deceit.'

Using the four preceding definitions, does killing the unborn by cutting them to pieces and selling their body parts fit the description of murder?

Does the legalization of marijuana fit the description of sorcery?

Does the mandate by the Supreme Court to recognize the marriage between two people of the same gender fit the description of sexual immorality?

Does the redistribution of wealth by way of taxation to fund activities performed by Planned Parenthood fit the description of thievery?

If any of the above practices or activities is not initiated or sanctioned by God, where do the thoughts for such legislation, Supreme Court decisions, or executive orders originate?

Who among you is wise and understanding? Let him show by his good behavior his deeds in the gentleness of wisdom. But if you have bitter jealousy and selfish ambition in your heart, do not be arrogant and so lie against the truth. This wisdom is not that which comes down from above, but is earthly, natural, demonic. James 3:13-15 NASB

God cannot lie

When considering all that is going on in the world, it is so comforting that we can always take God at His word. What He says, that He will do.

We never have to wonder where He stands. His word is immutable and eternal.

The following is a wonderful passage that contains several profound and relevant truths.

Paul, a bond-servant of God, and an apostle of Jesus Christ, for the faith of those chosen of God and the knowledge of the truth which is according to godliness, in the hope of eternal life, which God, who cannot lie, promised long ages ago, but at the proper time manifested, even His word... Titus 1:1-3 NASB

Even though Paul was an apostle of Jesus Christ, he humbly referred to himself as a bondservant. He acknowledged that Jesus was the truth that was promised before time began, but was kept a mystery until the age of the church.

The current relevant point is, however, that Paul acknowledged that God could not lie.

While God is truth and cannot lie, Satan is the father of lies. It's no wonder that the world is in chaos today.

The writer of Hebrews reiterated that great truth when describing God's promise to Abraham.

In the same way God, desiring even more to show to the heirs of the promise the unchangeableness of His purpose, interposed with an oath, in order that by two unchangeable things, in which it is impossible for God to lie...
Hebrews 6:17-18 NASB

The two immutable things were that God swore by Himself, and it was impossible for Him to lie.

Summary statement

The church age is certainly not immune to the works of the devil. The Bible reveals that satanic tactics are active not only during the church age, but also within the church itself.

The reasons for this are due to the reality of the presence of many within the church that are rejecters or pretenders, either by choice or by deceit.

The nations are being deceived in this current age as evidenced by their priorities.

God's wrath will fall on the deceived as well as the deceivers.

"...If any one worships the beast and his image, and receives a mark on his forehead or upon his hand, he also will drink of the wine of the wrath of God, which is mixed in

full strength in the cup of His anger; and he will be tormented with fire and brimstone in the presence of the holy angels and in the presence of the Lamb." Revelation 14:9-10 NASB

Praise God that He has made Himself known to us!

Chapter 6

Idolatry: Past, Present, and Future

Israel has a long history of idolatry. While idolatry has taken on many forms, its basic definition is to worship, or serve anything other than the one and true God.

An idol can be something tangible made with hands, or it can be an ideology or concept. In all cases it is an imaginary false deity (god).

To serve an idol of any kind is to commit spiritual adultery against God. These definitions basically apply to the Hebrew meanings of idolatry as well as to the Greek definitions found in the New Testament.

God writes history in advance

Just prior to Moses' death, God told him that Israel would be involved in idolatry to the extent that He would forsake them and hide His face from them, all because they would turn to other gods.

And the LORD said to Moses, "Behold, you are about to lie down with your fathers; and this people will arise and play the harlot with the strange gods of the land, into the midst of which they are going...and will forsake Me and break My covenant which I have made with them."
Deuteronomy 31:16 NASB

It is so amazing that Israel's Sovereign God would reveal the future thoughts and actions of His people.

The KJ version uses the phrasing 'go a whoring after the gods of the strangers of the land.' God had previously warned the Israelites on numerous occasions of the consequences of not completely ridding the land of its occupants.

In the present context the wording 'play the harlot' means to have illegal contact between Israel and other nations and their gods.

God was very specific relative to Israel's future actions and the required consequences. He instructed Moses to write down beforehand what they would do and use the writing, called a song, as a witness confirming His warning.

"...write this song ...and teach it to the sons of Israel... For when I bring then into the land...and they have eaten and are satisfied and become prosperous, then they will turn to other gods and serve them, and spurn Me and break My covenant." Deuteronomy 31:19-20 NASB

God told Moses in advance that the Israelites would be given everything they could possibly need or want, but instead of praising God for His goodness, they would give the credit for their success to false gods.

Perhaps they would credit their own ingenuity and effort for their success, or perhaps they would tout their trading treaties with other nations for their economic prowess. Whatever their reasoning, they would forget their true provider and 'worship' their self accomplishment. Such would become 'other gods.'

God also foretells the cost of disobedience

But just as God explained their behavior in advance, such apostasy would have disastrous results.

"Then it shall come about, when many evils and troubles have come upon them, that this song will testify before them as a witness...for I know their intent which they are developing today, before I have brought them into the land which I swore." Deuteronomy 31:21 NASB

After recording the words of the song in the book of the law and placing it in the Ark of the Covenant, Moses called the elders and officers together and told them what God had told him.

"For I know that after my death you will act corruptly and turn from the way which I have commanded you; and evil

will befall you in the latter days, for you will do that which is evil in the sight of the LORD, provoking Him to anger with the work of your hands." Deuteronomy 31:29 NASB

The Hebrew word for work in this context means 'labor, or something made,' while 'hands' means 'power or strength.' Thus, the Israelites would attribute all their success to their own efforts instead of God's grace.

The term 'in the latter days' has eschatological implications; God's justice has not, as yet, been fully levied on His chosen nation. Such will be accomplished during the 'time of Jacob's trouble,' i.e. the great tribulation.

It must always be kept in mind Paul's application of Israel's history, particularly during the forty years between the Exodus and entering the Promised Land.

Now these things happened to them as an example, and they were written for our instruction, upon whom the ends of the ages have come. 1 Corinthians 10:11 NASB

Contemporary idols for the 'world'

We've seen that God warned Israel about idolatry and its consequences before they even entered the Promised Land.

Let's go forward about half a millennium and resume the discussion.

The idols of the nations are but silver and gold, the work of man's hands. They have mouths, but they do not speak... eyes, but they do not see; they have ears, but they do not hear; nor is there any breath at all in their mouth. Those who make them will be like them, yes, (so is) everyone who trusts in them. Psalm 135:15-18 NASB

The idols referenced are those of the gentiles and are made of silver and gold. Both metals were considered valuable, then and especially now.

Idols are described as completely lifeless; they are totally impotent to do anything. Those who make them or trust in them are equally worthless.

Thereafter, the prophets spoke much about idols and the futility of dependence on them.

"Let them bring forth and declare to us what is going to take place...that we may consider them...or announce to us what is coming...that we may know that you are gods... behold, you are of no account, and your work amounts to nothing; he who chooses you is an abomination."
Isaiah 41:22-24 NASB

The challenges presented for idols to prove themselves are exclusively acts of deity. Only God can declare that which is to come and proclaim the end from the beginning. It is again declared that idols are nothing and he who trusts in such is an abomination, i.e. a detestable thing.

God admonishes His people to look only to Him for deliverance.

"Turn to Me, and be saved, all the ends of the earth; for I am God, and there is no other. I have sworn by Myself, the word has gone forth from My mouth in righteousness and will not turn back, that to Me every knee will bow, every tongue will swear allegiance." Isaiah 45:22-23 NASB

Truth prevails and is timeless. Nearly 800 years later the Apostle Paul echoed God's words.

Therefore also God highly exalted Him, and bestowed on Him the name which is above every name, that at the name of Jesus every knee should bow...and that every tongue should confess that Jesus Chris is Lord, to the glory of God the Father. Philippians 2:9-11 NASB

Who but God could proclaim the future in detail?

'Let your idols save you'

God foreknew all of Israel's history before time began. Back in the time of Moses, He proclaimed that the day would come when Israel would be in dire need of deliverance from their enemies.

"And He will say, 'Where are their gods, the rock in which they sought refuge? ...Let them rise up and help you, let them be your hiding place!'" Deuteronomy 32:37-38 NASB

God virtually mocks the idolaters by telling them to turn to their self-made idols in their time of troubles to deliver them from adversity.

Centuries later in the time of Isaiah, as in ages past, He derided those who trusted in idols.

"When you cry out, let your collection of idols deliver you. But the wind will carry all of them...away."
Isaiah 57:13 NASB

Only those who trusted in God would inherit the land in the time of the millennial kingdom. False gods, i.e. idols and those who trusted in them would be blown away by the wind into eternal separation from the only God.

Jeremiah likewise extolled the folly of idolatry.

Thus you shall say to them, "The gods that did not make the heavens and the earth shall perish from the earth and from under the heaven." It is He who made the earth by His power, who established the world by His wisdom; and by His understanding He has stretched out the heavens.
Jeremiah 10:11-12 NASB

God states that gods have no power of creation. Creation is exclusively an act of deity. God creates according to His purpose and discretion. The wisdom of God was embodied in Christ before the foundation of the world. Any other 'gods' shall perish.

God subsequently reminded Jeremiah that those of Judah and the city of Jerusalem have turned their backs on Him by serving other gods. They have broken the covenant God made with their fathers.

Therefore, thus says the LORD, "Behold I am bringing disaster on them which they will not be able to escape; though they will cry to Me, yet I will not listen to them." Jeremiah 11:11 NASB

Israel forsook their God for gods

Moses' final words provided specific details of the idolatry that Israel would be involved with when they entered and prospered in their Promised Land. They would mingle with the remnants of the gentiles that had not been deposed by Joshua. The result would be, in essence, multiculturalism. Such had been specifically warned against and forbidden.

Recall the Israelites had been instructed that there would be but one law for the Israelites and the strangers (aliens) remaining in the land.

God's prophetic warning would soon become reality.

The following passages from Deuteronomy 32 are written in the past tense even though written in advance of Israel entering the Promised Land.

"But Jeshurun (Israel) grew fat and kicked...then he forsook God who made him, and scorned the Rock of his salvation." Deuteronomy 32:15 NASB

Thus, when Israel had received the gifts provided by God (the Rock of their deliverance and victory) and prospered greatly in their new land, they became proud and set their Provider aside. They claimed full credit for their success.

Notice how their actions coincided with an earlier warning given during their forty years in the wilderness.

"Then it shall come about when the LORD your God brings you into the land which He swore to your fathers, Abraham, Isaac and Jacob, to give you, great and splendid cities which you did not build...and you shall eat and be satisfied, then watch yourself, lest you forget the LORD who brought you from the land of Egypt, out of the house of slavery." Deuteronomy 6:10-12 NASB

Moses stressed the fact that Israel had forgotten, i.e. willfully set aside, the source of their success.

"You neglected the Rock who begot you, and forgot the God who gave you birth." Deuteronomy 32:18

Paul defined the 'Rock' approximately fifteen centuries later.

For I do not want you to be unaware, brethren, that our fathers were all under the cloud, and all passed through the

sea; and all ate the same spiritual food; and all drank the same spiritual drink, for they were drinking from a spiritual rock which followed them; and the rock was Christ.
1 Corinthians 10:1-4 NASB

Idolatry will destroy a nation

Recall Jeremiah's final warning for those clinging to idolatry.

"Then the cities of Judah and the inhabitants of Jerusalem will go and cry to the gods to whom they burn incense, but they surely will not save them in the time of their disaster." Jeremiah 11:12 NASB

Idolatry has devastating consequences. God confirms that Judah and Jerusalem will cry out to their gods for deliverance; however, their gods are totally powerless to do anything.

"Therefore do not pray for this people, nor lift up a cry or prayer for them; for I will not listen when they call to Me because of their disaster." Jeremiah 11:14 NASB

Judah and Jerusalem had reached the point of no return. There was no remedy for them, but rather the foretold deportation to Babylon had arrived.

In current times many may attempt to compromise, i.e. claim to be citizens of the Kingdom while clinging to idols. Many times idols are not recognized as such.

Idols are false gods. They can represent anything that rules the thoughts and desires, whether tangible or a concept of the mind. As such they are imaginary deities and falsely worshipped.

Very simply stated, they are not God.

Just as God told Jeremiah not to pray for those who wouldn't forsake their idols, such applies to those in the latter days.

Idolaters will not inherit nor enjoy a part in the millennial kingdom; rather they will be raised to stand before the great white throne judgment.

"But for the cowardly and unbelieving and abominable and murderers and immoral persons and sorcerers and idolaters and all liars, their part will be in the lake that burns with fire and brimstone, which is the second death." Revelation 21:8 NASB

Likewise, such idolaters will not reside in the New Jerusalem which will descend out of heaven.

Outside are the dogs and the sorcerers and the immoral persons and the murderers and the idolaters, and everyone who loves and practices a lie. Revelation 22:15 NASB

While God will give freely from the fountain the waters of life to everyone who thirsts for it, the 'world' seeks to prepare for the future by assembling idols.

Only God can deliver from death. Only God can tell the end from the beginning. Only God is God.

The world, and particularly America, is in utter chaos. Many are claiming that the answer to survive through an uncertain future is to buy and hoard gold or silver.

God told the Israelites in the Old Testament that the idols of the nations were made of silver and gold. He reminded them that such were totally impotent to speak, see, or hear. They had no ability to provide wisdom or speak of future events. They were completely dead.

What can a thousand Krugerrands do to deliver a person from the righteous judgment of God?

Judah and Jerusalem would not forsake their idols until finally God told Jeremiah not to pray for them, inasmuch as they had passed the point of remedy.

The very same challenge faces America today, i.e. are we also so dependant on idols that we as a nation have passed the point of no return? Or do we even recognize the influence of idols surrounding us?

From manna to mammon

The following is a detailed example of an individual or nation departing from God's gracious provisions, and turning instead to the quest for more than God's providential care.

In less than two months after Israel was delivered from Egyptian bondage, they began to complain to Moses that they didn't have food to eat like they had in Egypt.

Then the LORD said to Moses, "Behold, I will rain bread from heaven for you..." Exodus 16:4 NASB

God established rules relating to the gathering of the bread (manna) to test the Israelite's faith in God's word that He would provide for their needs. Specifically, they were not to gather on the 7th day, but rather gather enough on the 6th day to last for two days.

Approximately three months after exiting Egypt, God issued His initial laws, beginning with the Ten Commandments.

The people responded:

...and all the people answered with one voice, and said, "All the words which the LORD has spoken we will do!" Exodus 24:3 NASB

Good intentions faded away

As history unfolded, the Israelites began to stray from God's laws and even made idols to worship in place of the true God.

As the forty year wilderness journey was about to come to a close, as the Israelites were about to cross the Jordan River, God told Moses in advance what they would do in the future. Moses was told to record God's words in a 'song.'

God foretold that after Israel prospered, they would turn from their Provider.

"They made Him jealous with strange gods; with abominations they provoked Him to anger. They sacrificed to demons who were not God, to gods whom they have not known, new gods who came lately, whom your fathers did not dread." Deuteronomy 32:16-17 NASB

Of course God would definitely redeem His people and forgive their sin, but not without severe chastisement.

Many years later David acknowledged the one, true God as he was looking into the latter days.

There is no one like Thee among the gods, O LORD; nor are there any works like Thine. All nations whom Thou hast made shall come and worship before Thee, O LORD; and they shall glorify Thy name...Thou alone art God.
Psalm 86:8-10 NASB

Isaiah, reaffirming God's words, subsequently repeated the great universal truth that there is but one God.

"Before Me there was no God formed, and there will be none after Me." Isaiah 43:10c NASB

'Formed' in this verse can be something tangible like silver or gold, or intangible like one's thoughts, purpose, or ideology.

One of the major reasons for northern Israel being overrun by Assyria in 722 BC was their idolatry.

And they rejected His statutes and His covenant which He made with their fathers...and they followed vanity...and went after the nations...which the LORD had commanded them not to do like them...they forsook all the commandments of the LORD their God and made for themselves molten images...2 Kings 17:15-16 NASB

Idols are gods

The psalmists stated that gods of the people are idols.

For great is the LORD, and greatly to be praised; He is to be feared above all gods, for all the gods of the peoples are idols, but the LORD made the heavens. Psalm 96:4-5 NASB

David had spoken the above words as he placed the Ark in the tent he had made for it in Jerusalem.

For all the gods of the peoples are idols, but the LORD made the heavens. 1 Chronicles 16:26 NASB

New Testament gods

Before beginning discourse about gods in the age of the church, let's not forget Paul's writing relative to the applicability of the Old Testament to the New.

Now these things happened to them as an example, and they were written for our instruction, upon whom the ends of the ages have come. 1 Corinthians 10:11 NASB

The most widely used Greek word for 'gods' in the New Testament is *daimon* meaning demon. Synonyms for *daimon* include 'false accuser,' or 'the devil.'

"...we know that an idol is nothing in the world...for us there is one God, the Father, of whom are all things, and we for Him; and one Lord Jesus Christ..."
1 Corinthians 8:4, 6 NKJV

Paul praised the church at Thessalonica because they had turned to God from idols, and led others to do the same.

...and how you turned to God from idols to serve a living and true God, and to wait for His Son from heaven...
1 Thessalonians 1:9-10 NASB

And though coveting doesn't appear to some to be a serious sin, the Bible states that coveting is a form of idolatry.

For this you know with certainty, that no immoral or impure person or covetous man, who is an idolater, has an inheritance in the kingdom of Christ and God.
Ephesians 5:5 NASB

'Idolater' in the present context means 'one who worships idols,' while 'covetous' means 'lover of silver or money.'

This truth is so significant that Paul taught it to the church at Colosse also.

Therefore consider the members of your earthly body as dead to immorality, impurity, passion, evil desires, and greed, which amounts to idolatry. Colossians 3:5 NASB

Paul states that one should put to death those parts of his being that lusts after earthly things, which includes idolatrous covetousness.

Perhaps John summed it up the most succinctly.

Little children, guard yourselves from idols. 1 John 5:21 NASB

Mammon is perhaps the most subtle idol confronting the world today

Jesus warned about mammon as did the apostle John in the final book of the Bible.

Jesus warned about the lust for wealth, and stated that those parts of the body that focus on things of the world should be eliminated. A person must choose between desiring (coveting) the corruptible things of the world, or those things that produce eternal rewards in the future.

"No one can serve two masters; for either he will hate the one and love the other, or he will hold to one and

despise the other. You cannot serve God and mammon."
Matthew 6:24 NASB

'Mammon' is described as 'the god of materialism.' Mammon is the personification of earthly riches and wealth.

Luke confirmed Jesus' message.

"No servant can serve two masters..." Luke 16:13 NASB

The meaning of 'servant' in this passage means, 'voluntary servitude.' In other words it applies to one who voluntary chooses the master that he desires to follow. Likewise 'serve' means 'will,' 'desire,' and 'intent.'

To have wealth by itself is not a sin; it is the motive behind obtaining wealth.

Recall, way back during the time of Israel's wilderness journey, the subject was addressed by God.

"But you shall remember the LORD your God, for it is He who is giving you power to make wealth, that He may confirm His covenant which He swore to your fathers, as it is this day. And it shall come about if you ever forget the LORD your God, and go after other gods and serve them and worship them, I testify against you today that you shall surely perish." Deuteronomy 8:18-19 NASB

The final Babylon

Just prior to Christ returning to earth to end the great tribulation, the mighty idolatrous city of Babylon, which represents the sum total of mammon, will fall, never to arise out of the flames forever.

A mighty angel describes the reason for her fall.

"For all the nations have drunk of the wine of the wrath of her fornication, the kings of the earth have committed fornication with her, and the merchants of the earth have become rich through the abundance of her luxury." Revelation 18:3 NKJV

The word 'abundance' means the cities' tremendous strength and power to influence the kings and merchants of the earth. The angel terms it 'fornication' inasmuch as fornication is spiritual adultery against almighty God.

'Luxury' or delicacies means 'lust' and 'pleasure.'

Men will abandon all reason and religion in favor of sensuality and pleasure.

The fate of the city and all its citizens will be destruction by fire. The city will burn and the citizens will end in the eternal lake of fire.

How is America doing?

Note the similarity of Israel's behavior and that of America.

America was once under the rule of another nation and was set free. America now touts that she is the most exceptional nation in the 'world' due to her ingenuity and economic prowess.

Now that America is experiencing economic challenges, and facing threats from 'those of the East,' is seeking God's deliverance her first priority?

What solutions were being offered by those seeking the office of president during the recent political chaos?

Does America seek the Rock, or their many rocks? Does America depend on missile defense systems to protect herself from the likes of North Korea or Iran? Does America depend on UN Sanctions to control the aggression of hostile nations? Does America strive for internal peace by passing legislation that protects those engaged in abominable practices?

Does America participate in multiculturalism to win the approval of other nations? Perhaps America should consult the Bible or simply ask Europe how that strategy is working.

Recent presidential aspirants contended that the first step in national success is to have a robust and growing economy. That is the accepted 'rock' for America to remain the most exceptional nation in the world.

God reveals the naiveté of such thinking.

"See now that I, I am He, and there is no god besides Me...and there is no one who can deliver from My hand." Deuteronomy 32:39 NASB

God is the 'Rock' and the only power to deliver victory from enemies. His plan for the nations and His purpose for His chosen will stand.

Many are beginning to think that Franklin Graham is right by disassociating himself from any political faction and turning directly to God for America's future.

Of course he's right.

We always need to keep in mind Paul's admonition to the church when he stated that those things that happened to Israel, especially during their receiving the law prior to entering the Promised Land, serve as examples for us in this current age.

What are America's priorities?

The consequences of idolatry and the coveting of mammon should cause all to pause and consider several issues.

- What are America's primary goals?

- What are the major tenets of the American Dream?

- Is America in sync with Biblical truths?

- Is it meaningful, or mockery for our presidents to say 'God bless America' at the end of State of the Union addresses?

Exciting times lie ahead.

Chapter 7

Church Age Suffering and Persecution

The Christian cherishes suffering (affliction) as a non-regiftable blessing, because such suffering for the sake of Christ in like manner represents the suffering He did for us.

Peter expressed those thoughts wonderfully.

Beloved, do not be surprised at the fiery ordeal among you, which comes upon you for your testing, as though some strange thing were happening to you; but to the degree that you share the sufferings of Christ, keep on rejoicing; so that also at the revelation of His glory you may rejoice with exultation. 1 Peter 4:12-13 NASB

Suffering, in the eyes of the Christian, represents an intimate relationship with Jesus Christ that began before the foundation of the world.

...just as He chose us in Him before the foundation of the world, that we should be holy and blameless before Him. He predestined us to adoption as sons through Jesus

Christ to Himself, according to the kind intention of His will... Ephesians 1:4-5 NASB

Paul confirms that not only is faith a gift of God, so is suffering for Christ's sake.

For to you it has been granted for Christ's sake, not only to believe in Him, but also to suffer for His sake... Philippians 1:29 NASB

Christ and his followers are inseparable

When writing to the Christians in Rome, Paul said that believers are children of God; and suffering with Christ has as its ultimate future reward to be given a glorified body as Christ has now.

...and if children, heirs also, heirs of God and fellow-heirs with Christ, if indeed we suffer with Him in order that we may also be glorified with Him. Romans 8:17 NASB

Paul goes on to state than nothing can separate the Christian from the love of God 'which is in Christ Jesus our Lord.'

Who shall separate us from the love of Christ? Shall tribulation, or distress, or persecution...? Romans 8:35 NASB

Suffering will abound wherever Christianity is found

Peter tells those to whom he is writing that the suffering they are experiencing is being experienced by the Christian Brotherhood throughout the world.

But...(be)...firm in your faith, knowing that the same experiences of suffering are being accomplished by your brethren who are in the world. And after you have suffered for a little, the God of all grace, who called you to His eternal glory in Christ, will Himself perfect, confirm, strengthen and establish you. 1 Peter 5:9-10 NASB

In his letters to the church at Corinth, the apostle Paul reinforced Peter's message.

For just as the sufferings of Christ are ours in abundance, so also our comfort is abundant through Christ...and our hope for you is firmly grounded, knowing that as you are sharers of our sufferings, so also you are sharers of our comfort. 2 Corinthians 1:5, 7 NASB

As Christians partake of the sufferings of Christ, they will likewise partake of the consolation (comfort) which abounds through Christ. The Greek for 'consolation,' or comfort, is *parakletos* which was the term used by Jesus when He announced the coming of the Holy Spirit to His disciples.

Rewards for suffering

Paul further addresses the rewards of his personal suffering.

Now I rejoice in my sufferings for your sake, and in my flesh I do my share on behalf of His body (which is the church) in filling up that which is lacking in Christ's afflictions. Colossians 1:24 NASB

All Christians have either suffered in the past, are suffering in the present, or will suffer in the future. Suffering for the Christian is a gift to all true believers.

Many examples of suffering are illustrated in the Bible. Consider Peter and the apostles in the early days of the church. After refusing to cease speaking the truth about Christ, they were punished repeatedly by the Sadducees led by the high priest.

After one such beating, Peter and the apostles' response was:

So they went on their way from the presence of the Council, rejoicing that they had been considered worthy to suffer shame for His name. Acts 5:41 NASB

The 'world' considers this passage to be utterly foolish. But for the Christian to suffer is to partake in the sufferings of Christ. Such suffering confirms the presence of the Holy Spirit and in turn glorifies God.

The Greek for 'suffering' in the above has many synonyms including 'sickness,' 'misery,' 'affliction,' or 'wounds.'

But consider the end result.

And we proclaim Him, admonishing every man and teaching every man with all wisdom, that we may present every man complete (perfect) in Christ.
Colossians 1:28 NASB

The objective is for every follower to be complete (perfect) in Christ.

The Greek for 'perfect' (complete) means 'whole,' 'finish,' and 'goal.' In other words, suffering for Christians will fulfill God's purpose for which they were created.

The apostles stressed the glory involved in suffering for the sake of Christ, and Paul also put that suffering in perspective within the big picture.

For I consider that the sufferings of this present time are not worthy to be compared with the glory that is to be revealed in us. Romans 8:18 NASB

Therefore, the Christian should be prepared to experience suffering and endure all suffering with deep confidence, peace and joy.

Suffering in the flesh; however, may be due to disobedience

Physical suffering can be caused by disobedience to God's commands.

Recall the word to the Israelites just prior to entering the Promised Land.

"But it shall come about, if you will not obey the LORD your God to observe to do all His commandments and His statutes which I charge you today, that all these curses shall come upon you and overtake you..."
Deuteronomy 28:15 NASB

Though there are many, we'll mention just a sampling.

"The LORD will smite you...with hemorrhoids and with the scab and with the itch, from which you cannot be healed." Deuteronomy 28:27 NASB

"The LORD will strike you on the knees and legs with sore boils...from the sole of your foot to the crown of your head." Deuteronomy 28:35 NASB

Boils were open, festered sores, seeping fluids.

"If you are not careful to observe all the words of this law...then the LORD will bring extraordinary plagues on you and your descendants, even severe and lasting plagues, and miserable and chronic sicknesses."
Deuteronomy 28:58-59 NASB

'Plagues' refer to slaughter and wounds, while 'sicknesses' refers to infirmity and pain.

And God may inflict suffering for disobedience, in ways that have not been revealed in Scripture.

"And He will bring back on you all the diseases of Egypt of which you were afraid, and they shall cling to you...Also every sickness and every plague which, not written in the book of this law, the LORD will bring on you until you are destroyed." Deuteronomy 28:60-61 NASB

Suffering may be permitted to prove one's faithfulness

When God permitted the devil to cause Job to suffer, the infliction resembled the curse on the disobedience of Israel.

Then Satan went out from the presence of the LORD, and smote Job with sore boils from the sole of his foot to the crown of his head. Job 2:7 NASB

Job expressed in his own words the magnitude of his pain.

"My flesh is caked with worms (maggots) and dust, my skin is cracked and breaks out afresh." Job 7:5 NKJV

But then, recall God's restoration to Job for his faithfulness.

And the LORD restored the fortunes of Job...and the LORD increased all that Job had twofold...and the LORD blessed the latter days of Job more than his beginning... Job 42:10, 23 NASB

Restoration in this life isn't guaranteed; however, restoration sometime in the future is.

Suffering may be endured to bring glory to God

Recall the story of the man blind since birth. Many witnessed the miracle of Jesus when He restored sight to the blind man.

Their seemingly logical question was who sinned to cause the man to be blind in the first place.

Jesus answered, "It was neither that this man sinned, nor his parents; but it was in order that the works of God might be displayed in him." John 9:3 NASB

Similarly, Jesus' friend Lazarus became sick. His sisters, Mary and Martha sent word to Jesus that His friend was sick.

But when Jesus heard it, He said, "This sickness is not unto death, but for the glory of God, that the Son of God may be glorified by it." John 11:4 NASB

Jesus tarried for two more days before going to Bethany where Lazarus lived. Before Jesus arrived at Bethany, Lazarus died.

His sister Martha told Jesus that if He had been there, her brother would not have died.

Jesus said to her, "Did I not say to you, if you believe, you will see the glory of God?" John 11:40 NASB

And when He had said these things, He cried out with a loud voice, "Lazarus, come forth." He who had died came forth... John 11:43-44a NASB

And the purpose of the death of Lazarus, and his return to life was to glorify God.

Many therefore of the Jews...beheld what He had done, believed in Him. John 11:45 NASB

Suffering in the form of persecution

Christ told that suffering would be part of following Him during the church age preceding the tribulation.

"But before all these things, they will lay their hands on you and will persecute you, delivering you to the synagogues and prisons, bringing you before kings and governors for My name's sake. It will lead to an opportunity for your testimony." Luke 21:12-13 NASB

Suffering persecution will present the Christian the opportunity to be a witness to those who persecute them.

And Jesus declared that those who are willing to give up everything held in esteem in this life will be granted that which they are willing to give up; however, such will be accompanied with persecution.

Jesus said, "Truly I say to you, there is no one who has left house or brothers or sisters or mother or father or children or farms, for My sake and for the gospel's sake, but that he shall receive a hundred times as much now in the present age, houses and brothers and sisters and mothers and children and farms, along with persecutions; and in the world (age) to come, eternal life." Mark 10:29-30 NASB

"But seek first His kingdom and His righteousness; and all these things shall be added to you." Matthew 6:33 NASB

Yes, the Christian considers suffering to be a gift with indescribable rewards.

Persecution – a sure thing for Christians

The enemies of Christ hadn't had their fill of persecuting Christ so they turned their persecution on Christ's followers, the church.

There are few absolutes in this chaotic world, but it is certain that Christians will experience persecution. Once again we'll see that the world's majority are the persecutors while the kingdom minority is the persecuted.

Inasmuch as New Testament persecution is directed towards Jesus Christ, and Jesus is the head of the church, the church (Christians) will likewise be the object of persecution.

"Remember the word that I said to you, 'A slave is not greater than his master.' If they persecuted Me, they will also persecute you..." John 15:20 NASB

Paul confirmed that Christ's followers would be the recipients of persecution.

And indeed, all who desire to live godly in Christ Jesus will be persecuted. 2 Timothy 3:12 NASB

The Greek for 'persecution' in the above passage is *dioko.* The basic meaning of a persecutor is one who pursues another with repeated acts of enmity. Additional synonyms include, 'distress,' 'press,' 'crush,' 'against,' and/ or 'to follow after.' Persecution then, is ongoing, relentless, hostile activity.

Dealing with the inevitable

It has been established that persecution of Christians is inevitable and will persist until Christ returns to put an end to it. The Bible teaches how to deal with persecution and the persecutor.

"Blessed are you when men revile you, and persecute you, and say all kinds of evil against you falsely, on account of Me. Rejoice, and be glad, for your reward in heaven is great for so they persecuted the prophets who were before you." Matthew 4:11-12 NASB

The Greek for 'Blessed' in the above passage means 'possessing the favor of God.'

To be reviled and persecuted for Jesus' sake is evidence that one is in the hands of God. The Christian is to rejoice while being persecuted with great confidence that such persecution will result in heavenly rewards. The Christian is then told that others of God's chosen suffered persecution prior to the church. God's chosen includes the 'Apple of His eye,' i.e. national Israel.

In his first letter to the church in Thessalonica, Paul reiterates the inevitableness of suffering and encourages perseverance.

*...so that no man may be disturbed by these afflictions; for you yourselves know that we have been destined (appointed) for this. For indeed when we were with you, we kept telling you in advance that we were going to suffer affliction; and so it came to pass...*1 Thessalonians 3:3-4 NASB

Note in particular that Christians have been destined (appointed) to suffer which means that suffering is in integral part of being a Christian.

Jesus had previously instructed His followers how to respond to their persecutors.

"But I say to you, love your enemies, and pray for those who persecute you..." Matthew 5:44 NASB

The Christian is not to retaliate for the wrongs done to him; rather the response should be to invoke God's best on them.

The Greek for 'bless' in the above passage does in fact mean to 'invoke God's blessings' on one's persecutors.

Later Paul expounded on Jesus' teachings when dealing with persecutors.

Bless those who persecute you; bless and curse not. Romans 12:14 NASB

...when we are reviled, we bless; when we are persecuted, we endure... 1 Corinthians 4:12 NASB

Paul confirmed Jesus' teachings, i.e. Christians are admonished to love their enemies and persevere in the presence of persecution.

The persecutor became the persecuted

Persecution against the early church was poignantly illustrated by the activities of the Pharisee named Saul. At the time of Stephen's death, the church was experiencing great persecution.

And on that day (of Stephan's death) a great persecution arose against the church in Jerusalem...but Saul began ravaging the church, entering house after house; and dragging off men and women, he would put them in prison.
Acts 8:1, 3 NASB

Saul was shortly thereafter confronted by Jesus on the road to Damascus relative to his activities.

...and he (Saul) fell to the ground, and heard a voice saying to him, "Saul, Saul, why are you persecuting Me?...I am Jesus whom you are persecuting." Acts 9:4-5 NASB

As the story unfolds, Jesus revealed that the chief persecutor of the church would become the chief persecuted of the church.

But the Lord said to him, "Go, for he is a chosen instrument of Mine, to bear My name before the Gentiles and the kings and the sons of Israel; for I will show him how much he must suffer for My name's sake."
Acts 9:15-16 NASB

Saul was a 'chosen vessel' which means he and his mission was appointed before the foundation of the world. His Hebrew name was subsequently changed to his Roman name, which is Paul, and we know the rest of the story.

Saul persecuted Jesus and the church before meeting Him and the Father. Jesus had forewarned His disciples that such would happen.

"They will make you outcasts from the synagogue; but an hour is coming for everyone who kills you to think that he is offering service to God. And these things they will do, because they have not known the Father, or Me. But these things I have spoken to you, that when their hour comes, you may remember that I told you of them." John 16:2-4 NASB

There were many then, and there are many now in the church that have been deceived, i.e. they are not really the called of Christ. Such will not endure persecution and their true identity will be revealed.

The target of the persecutors

Jesus taught the multitudes four different classifications of those who would hear about the kingdom of God. The different groups were referred to as 'soils.' Some seeds (God's word) would fall by the wayside, some would fall on stony places, and some would fall among thorns and some on good ground and would yield a crop.

Of current interest in the context of persecution is the seed that fell on stony places. Jesus later explained the meaning of the parable to His disciples.

"But he who received the seed on stony places, this is he who hears the word and immediately receives it with joy; yet he has no root in himself, but endures only for a while. For when tribulation or persecution arises...immediately he stumbles." Matthew 13:20-21 NKJV

Thus, of the four types of soils, the seed prospered in just one type, i.e. the 'good ground.' And remember, Jesus taught His disciples that the path leading to life was narrow while the path leading to destruction was wide.

The Bible explicitly tells how the Christian is to deal with persecution, the rewards awaiting those who suffer inevitable persecution, and the punishment for the persecutors.

Identifying the persecutors

In his letter to the church in Galatia, Paul revealed the source of persecution for God's chosen.

While the two divisions of mankind are generally defined as either belonging to the 'world,' or being members of the 'kingdom,' Paul defines the two classifications as either being 'born according to the flesh,' or being 'born according to the Spirit.'

For it is written that Abraham had two sons, one by the bondwoman and one by the free woman. But the son by the bondwoman was born according to the flesh, and

the son by the free woman through the promise...And you brethren, like Isaac, are children of promise. But as at that time he who was born according to the flesh persecuted him who was born according to the Spirit, so it is now also. Galatians 4:22-23, 28-29 NKJV

Therefore, according to Paul, those born according to the flesh depend on salvation by works. Those born according to the Spirit, i.e. children of promise, believe salvation is a gift based on the vicarious sacrifice of Christ.

Note particularly that Ishmael represents the offspring of the bondwoman while Isaac represents the offspring of the freewoman. Then Paul notes that Ishmael persecuted Isaac approximately 2000 years before the church, and such persecution existed during Paul's day.

And then Paul confirmed that the church consisted of children of the freewoman, but the offspring of the bondwoman was to be 'cast out.' The two divisions had nothing in common.

"Nevertheless what does the Scripture say? 'Cast out the bondwoman and her son, for the son of the bondwoman shall not be heir with the son of the freewoman.' So then, brethren, we are not children of the bondwoman but of the free." Galatians 4:30-31 NKJV

Now remember Ishmael and his bondwoman mother were sent to the East as was his offspring.

In these days, where is the greatest persecution of God's chosen, the church and national Israel, being perpetrated in the world today? Is it not in the Middle East?

Such gross persecution will be present as long as the brothers continue to battle.

"And he will be a wild donkey of a man, his hand will be against everyone, and everyone's hand will be against him; and he will live to the east of all his brothers."
Genesis 16:12 NASB

Do America's leaders really have a grasp of the significance of the conflict in the Middle East, or do they naively think those nations can be reconciled via diplomacy?

Jesus said the hypocritical Pharisees were no different than their fathers

Persecution directed at the seed of Abraham and Isaac has increased during the centuries and will accelerate as the end of the church age approaches.

The historical books of the Bible reveal that just prior to the Babylonian captivity, apostate Jews persecuted God's prophets to the extent that judgment was inevitable.

And the LORD, the God of their fathers, sent word to them again and again by His messengers, because He had compassion of His people...but they continually mocked the

messengers of God, despised His words and scoffed at His prophets, until there was no remedy.
2 Chronicles 36:15-16 NASB

Mocking, despising, and scoffing of the prophets by the unrepentant are the same actions that described Ishmael's persecution of Isaac.

Persecution of God's chosen continued relentlessly throughout the history of Israel and the church. Jesus condemned the Pharisees for their past and present hypocrisy regarding the persecution of the prophets.

"Woe to you, scribes and Pharisees, hypocrites! For you build the tombs of the prophets and adorn the monuments of the righteous, and say, 'If we had been living in the days of our fathers, we would not have been partners with them in shedding the blood of the prophets.'"
Matthew 23:29-30 NASB

Jesus unveiled their hypocrisy and confronted them with the truth.

"Consequently you bear witness against yourselves, that you are sons of those who murdered the prophets... Therefore, behold, I am sending you prophets and wise men and scribes; some of them you will kill and crucify, and some of them you will scourge in your synagogues, and persecute from city to city..." Matthew 23:31, 34 NASB

The persecution of the church in the present age is basically a continuation of the persecution of God's people in previous ages. All persecution was/is focused on Jesus Christ and God's chosen.

Recall Stephen's words just prior to his death.

"You men who are stiff-necked and uncircumcised in heart and ears are always resisting the Holy Spirit; you are doing just as your fathers did. Which one of the prophets did your father not persecute? And they killed those who had previously announced the coming of the Righteous One, whose betrayers and murderers you have now become..."
Acts 7:51-52 NASB

Persecution has just been passed on to succeeding generations and will continue until the Object of persecution returns to end it.

In God's perfect timing, His required wrath will be unleashed on the persecutors and rewards given to the persecuted.

Justice for the persecuted and the persecutor

Consider God's promise to the persecuted:

...we...speak proudly of you among the churches of God for your perseverance and faith in the midst of all your persecutions and afflictions which you endure...so that you may be considered worthy of the kingdom of God, for

which indeed you are suffering. For after all it is only just for God...to give relief to you who are afflicted...when the Lord Jesus shall be revealed from heaven with His mighty angels in flaming fire... 2 Thessalonians 1:4-7 NASB

Now consider God's required wrath on the persecutor:

And these will pay the penalty of eternal destruction, away from the presence of the Lord and from the glory of His power... 2 Thessalonians 1:9 NASB

Every person is, by their own choice, a member of one of the two groups.

On the global scene, has America become a persecutor of Israel? And if so, what are the inevitable consequences?

And why is Christianity the most persecuted religion in the world?

Understanding the history and significance of Isaac and Ishmael (and their descendants) will help explain the persecuted and persecutors along with their respective futures.

The reasons for all suffering may not always be obvious

Peter stated that God isn't glorified when we suffer the consequences for things we have done, but He is glorified, and we are blessed, when we suffer for the sake of Christ.

If you are reviled for the name of Christ, you are blessed, because the Spirit of glory and of God rests upon you. By no means let any of you suffer as a murderer, or thief, or evildoer, or a troublesome meddler; but if anyone suffers as a Christian, let him not feel ashamed, but in that name let him glorify God. 1 Peter 4:14-16 NASB

Or perhaps, suffering is the result of more subtle reasons.

"For he who eats and drinks in an unworthy manner eats and drinks judgment to himself, not discerning the Lord's body. For this reason many are weak and sick among you, and many sleep (are dead)." 1 Corinthians 11:29-30 NKJV

To summarize, all suffering is under the sovereign and watchful eye of Almighty God. Christians may not always understand their suffering; however, God knows perfectly well why we suffer, and suffering cannot exceed the limits that He has established.

Chapter 8

The King of Tyre

Tyre was an ancient city on the eastern shore of the Mediterranean Sea known for mercantilism and international trade activities. The recorded history of Tyre dates back to 2750 BC. Tyre became the major trading hub for eastern nations.

Tyre was more specifically located in the northern part of Canaan which was also known as the southern part of Phoenicia.

From Tyre to Tarshish, and back

Now travel west approximately 2,000 miles to the city of Tarshish, a seaport on the southwestern shores of Spain.

It will be revealed that Tyre and Tarshish form an intertwined commercial partnership.

Tarshish is first mentioned in the Bible as originating from the lineage of Noah's son Japheth.

*"The sons of Japheth...Javan...and the sons of Javan...
Tarshish..."* Genesis 10:2, 4 NASB

The known history of Tarshish dates back to 3000 BC and was considered to be the western most city and port mentioned in the Bible.

Perhaps Tarshish's far distant location from Nineveh was the reason Jonah boarded a ship and headed there.

*"But Jonah arose to flee to Tarshish **from the presence of the LORD**."* Jonah 1:3a NKJV (emphasis mine)

Note the profundity of this passage, i.e. Jonah fled to Tarshish to distance himself from the presence of the LORD. We'll see that much more is involved than geographic distance.

Tarshish was an epithet for merchant vessels, inasmuch as large merchant ships utilized its port.

The large ships of Tarshish provided gold, silver, iron, tin, ivory, and lead to the east, predominantly Tyre, and her sister city Sidon, located to the north of Tyre on the eastern shore of the Mediterranean Sea.

Israel's kings traded extensively with Tarshish

*And all King Solomon's drinking vessels were of gold...
for the king had ships which went to Tarshish...once every*

three years the ships of Tarshish came bringing gold...
2 Chronicles 9:20a, 21 NASB

Tarshish was such a popular merchant port that a later king of Judah allied with the king of Israel to trade with Tarshish.

...Jehoshaphat king of Judah allied himself with Ahaziah king of Israel. He acted wickedly in so doing. So he allied himself with him to make ships to go to Tarshish...
2 Chronicles 20:35-36 NASB

However, to ally with wickedness for the sake of commercialism displeased God.

"Because you have allied yourself with Ahaziah, the LORD had destroyed your works." So the ships were broken and could not go to Tarshish. 2 Chronicles 20:37 NASB

God condemned idolatry in all forms, and Tarshish was mentioned as a source of materials for idols.

But they (idolatrous Israelites) are altogether stupid and foolish in their discipline of delusion – their idol is wood! Beaten silver is brought from Tarshish...
Jeremiah 10:8-9a NASB

When God subsequently explained to his prophets the judgment of Tyre, He listed their dealings with Tarshish as the primary reason for their fall.

Tyre came to represent a ruthless materialistic commercial center. When Tyre would fall, Tarshish would feel the loss also. Isaiah told of the tie between the two when he described Tyre's demise.

The oracle concerning Tyre. Wail, O ships of Tarshish, for Tyre is destroyed...for your stronghold is destroyed. Isaiah 23:1, 14 NASB

Approximately a century later Ezekiel reiterated the association between Tyre and Tarshish.

"Tarshish was your merchant because of your many luxury goods. They gave you silver, iron, tin, and lead for your goods." Ezekiel 27:12 NKJV

Thus, Tyre and Tarshish are inextricably intertwined.

The young lions of Tarshish

And then an extremely interesting mention of Tarshish is found later in the prophecy of Ezekiel.

The context is Tarshish's response to the great battle of the eastern nations against Israel during the great tribulation. Seven of the ten nations attacking Israel are listed, and then Tarshish is mentioned.

"Sheba, Dedan, the merchants of Tarshish, and all their young lions will say to you, 'Have you come to take plunder...?'" Ezekiel 38:13 NKJV

The merchant nations of Sheba, Dedan, and Tarshish are not directly involved in the plunder of Israel; however, they question the intent of the plunderers.

The Hebrew meaning of the 'young lions' of Tarshish has several definitions.

A popular interpretation is that the 'young lions' represent the offspring of Tarshish, i.e. other nations that will arise further to the west that espouse the concept of international trade, such as the Americas.

In days of old the ships of Tarshish were merchant vessels that delivered coveted merchandise to the east so the recipients could live in luxury and make idols of the merchandise.

Such a practice brought on the wrath of God. In future days, however, God will use merchant ships for good.

"The sons of foreigners shall build up your walls, and their kings shall minister to you...and the ships of Tarshish will come first, to bring your sons from afar, their silver and their gold with them, to the name of the LORD your God." Isaiah 60:9-10 NKJV

Now we'll shift the focus back to Tyre.

Tyre, a friend to Israel's kings

During the days of King David and his son Solomon, Tyre was a close ally of Israel.

After reigning seven years in Hebron, David assumed the kingship of all Israel, and he moved to Jerusalem where he desired to build a palace for himself. The year was 1002 BC.

Hiram, the king of Tyre, contacted David to offer assistance and materials.

Then Hiram king of Tyre sent messengers to David with cedar trees and carpenters and stonemasons; and they built a house for David. 2 Samuel 5:11 NASB

Then approximately thirty six years later when Solomon was anointed as king, Hiram contacted Solomon to offer assistance in building a house (temple) for the LORD.

Now Hiram king of Tyre sent his servants to Solomon, when he heard that they had anointed him king in place of his father, for Hiram had always been a friend of David. 1 Kings 5:1 NASB

Solomon responded by confirming to Hiram that God had forbidden his father David to build a temple because he had been a man of war. Solomon went on to say that God had given him rest and peace from his enemies and it was time to build a temple for God.

"And behold, I intend to build a house for the name of the LORD my God, as the LORD spoke to David my father, saying, 'Your son, whom I will set on your throne in your place, he will build the house for My name.'" 1 Kings 5:5 NASB

Hiram was delighted when he heard Solomon's response.

"Blessed be the LORD today, who has given to David a wise son over this great people." 1 Kings 5:7 NASB

And so it was, an agreement was made whereby Solomon's servants, along with Hiram's servants, would begin by cutting cedars from Lebanon.

During the early years of Solomon's reign he was also assisted by Hiram's sea servants.

King Solomon also built a fleet of ships...and Hiram sent his servants with the fleet, sailors who knew the sea, along with servants of Solomon. 1 Kings 9:26-27 NASB

Everything was fine; Solomon was given assistance when and where needed; and Hiram, the king of Tyre, gained much business trade and riches.

From friend to foe

But as time passed, Solomon died and the kingdom was divided in 931 BC into north and south. Tyre's king Hiram had also died.

Then in 874 BC, while Asa was king of Judah, Ahab became the king of Israel.

Ahab was an evil king. Not only was he evil; he married a foreigner.

"And it came to pass...that he (Ahab) took as wife Jezebel the daughter of Ethbaal, king of the Sidonians; and he went and served Baal and worshiped him. Then he set up an altar for Baal in the temple of Baal...and Ahab made a wooden image." 1 Kings 16:31-32 NKJV

This was absolutely a marriage for political purposes. Ethbaal, meaning 'Baal lives,' was the king who had subsequently replaced Hiram. The Sidonians included both Tyre and Sidon.

So the constructive relationship between Israel and Tyre had come to an end. Good king Hiram of Tyre was replaced with evil king Ethbaal, an idolater and the father-in-law of Israel's evil king Ahab. Ahab and his wife Jezebel would practice idolatry throughout Israel.

Thus Ahab did more to provoke the LORD God of Israel than all the kings of Israel who were before him. 1 Kings 16:33 NASB

At this point, Tyre became an idolatrous city, steeped in harlotry and riches.

Tyre's trading partners and their merchandise

The varied nations and people groups that traded specific merchandise with Tyre will be listed, inasmuch as it will relate directly to the future.

- Tarshish was your merchant because of your many luxury goods. They gave you silver, iron, tin, and lead...

- Present day Turkey traded in human lives, horses and mules.

- Dedan in Arabia traded ivory tusks, ebony, and items used for horse riders.

- Syria traded emeralds, corals, rubies, and cloth items.

- Judah and Israel traded agriculture items such as wheat, honey, and oil.

- Damascus traded for many luxury items of wine.

- Dan and Javan traded such items as wrought iron.

- Arabia traded lambs, rams, and goats.

- Sheba and Raamah in Arabia traded items of choicest spices, precious stones, and gold.

- Cities of Mesopotamia traded choice items in purple clothes, embroidered garments, and multicolored apparel.

As revealed, countries and people groups from Tarshish and all around the eastern shores of the Mediterranean Sea traded with Tyre.

The nations and people groups that traded with Tyre were from the western area of present day Turkey, east to present day Iran, south through Arabia, to northern Africa. Other specific trade partners included areas in Syria, Mesopotamia, Israel, and Egypt.

Common adjectives found describing traded items included 'choicest,' 'abundant,' 'luxury, 'precious,' and 'fine.' The items predominately centered on riches and wealth.

Tyre rejoiced over Judah's woes

Recall the events of 586 BC. Jerusalem and Judah had been overrun by Nebuchadnezzar, king of Babylon. Tyre reacted to the devastation of Jerusalem and Judah.

"...because Tyre has said concerning Jerusalem, 'Aha, the gateway of the peoples is broken; it has opened to me. I shall be filled, now that she is laid waste'" Ezekiel 26:2 NASB

Tyre thought that she would benefit from Jerusalem's fall by being the center of trade in the region; however, she was not aware of God's plan.

At this point God pronounces doom on Tyre and explains the reasons for His imminent actions, along with exact details of His plan. In the present context, the reason for God's judgment on Tyre was her treatment and attitude toward Israel.

The other reasons for God's judgment of Tyre will be expanded as we progress.

The proclamation of Tyre's fall

All was going very well…

For Tyre built herself a fortress and piled up silver like dust, and gold like the mire of the streets. Zechariah 9:3 NASB

And again, Tarshish is mentioned as a critical contributor to Tyre's success.

"The ships of Tarshish were the carriers for your merchandise. And you were filled and were very glorious in the heart of the seas. Your rowers have brought you into great waters…" Ezekiel 27:25-26a NASB

"…but the east wind broke you in the midst of the seas." Ezekiel 27:26b NKJV

Subsequently all the merchants involved with Tyre would fall.

"Your wealth, your ware, your merchandise, your sailors, and your pilots, your repairers of seams, your dealers in merchandise, and all your men of war who are in you, with all your company that is in your midst, will fall into the heart of the seas on the day of your overthrow."
Ezekiel 27:27 NASB

Tyre's fall would have a disastrous affect on many nations and peoples. All would be astonished that such a powerful trade system could fail.

"When your wares went out from the seas, you satisfied many peoples; with the abundance of your wealth and your merchandise you enriched the kings of earth."
Ezekiel 27:33 NASB

Tyre's merchandising system had made many leaders in varied countries rich through trading luxury goods; however, that very mercantilist system had turned her and her trading partners to idolatry, harlotry and pride.

"Who has taken this counsel against Tyre, the crowning city, whose merchants are princes, whose traders are the honorable of the earth? The LORD of hosts has purposed it, to bring to dishonor the pride of all glory, to bring into contempt all the honorable of the earth." Isaiah 23:8-9 NKJV

The priorities of Tyre and her trading partners had been turned upside down. Their judgment had been written and sealed.

Tyre's fall would be a wakeup call to the kings of the earth, and they would be terrified that such a thing could happen to a system that seemed so powerful and beneficial.

Do the nations of the world today see any relevance in Tyre's fate?

God announces explicit details of Tyre's fall

"...therefore, thus says the Lord GOD, 'Behold, I am against you, O Tyre, and I will bring up many nations against you, as the sea brings up its waves.'" Ezekiel 26:3 NASB

God reveals His plan in explicit terms. It is naïve for any world leader to use the phrase 'I will.' It is only God who can say 'I will' and have the power and authority to back it up.

Tyre consisted of villages on the mainland of Phoenicia along with an island city/fortress located about 1,200 feet off shore.

God had said that Tyre would eventually be covered by the sea, and so it was.

"'She will be a place for the spreading of nets in the midst of the sea, for I have spoken,' declares the Lord God, 'and she will become spoil for the nations.'" Ezekiel 26:5 NASB

The specific nations that God would bring against Tyre are Babylon and Greece.

For thus says the Lord God, "Behold, I will bring upon Tyre from the north Nebuchadnezzar king of Babylon...He will slay your daughters on the mainland with the sword; and he will make siege walls against you..." Ezekiel 26:7-8 NASB

As specific details are laid out, God confirms that Nebuchadnezzar's actions against Tyre were in part retaliation for their actions against His people.

"Also they will make a spoil of your riches and a prey of your merchandise, break down your walls..." Ezekiel 26:12 NASB

While 'riches' in this verse does mean 'wealth,' it is also synonymous with 'power' and 'strength.'

'Merchandise' in the above is a word that we'll note numerous times in the future, means 'traffic,' 'trade,' or 'to travel for trade.' The concept of trade, or materialism, is at the heart of ultimate idolatry and spiritual adultery.

Tyre's trading partner's response

Thus says the Lord GOD to Tyre, "Shall not the coastlands shake at the sound of your fall when the wounded groan, when the slaughter occurs in your midst?" Ezekiel 26:15 NASB

The nations surrounding Tyre will be astounded that such a powerful commercial center can be so decimated and brought to nothing.

The leaders of the other benefactors of Tyre's merchandising will pause and reflect on such events. They are totally humbled.

"Then all the princes of the sea will go down from their thrones, remove their robes...they will clothe themselves with trembling; they will sit on the ground, tremble every moment, and be appalled at you." Ezekiel 26:16 NASB

'Prince' means 'governor,' 'chief,' or 'king.'

The leaders of the surrounding nations cannot believe what they are seeing.

They will offer together a lament for Tyre.

"...How you have perished, O inhabited one, (by seafaring men), O renowned city, which was mighty on the sea, she and her inhabitants, who imposed her terror on all her inhabitants...Now the coastlands will tremble on the day of your fall; yes, the coastlands which are by the sea will be terrified at your passing." Ezekiel 26:17-18 NASB

The term 'seafaring men' relates primarily to those adept at operating on the Mediterranean Sea. It brings to mind those who traveled to and fro between Tyre and Tarshish.

'Renowned' means to be 'praised' or 'glorified.' If it could happen to Tyre, it could happen to any haughty nation.

"All the inhabitants of the isles (countries) will be astonished at you; their kings will be greatly afraid, and their countenance will be troubled." Ezekiel 27:35 NKJV

'Astonished' means to be 'devastated,' or stunned,' while 'greatly afraid' or 'sore afraid' means to 'bristle with terror,' or to be 'horribly afraid.'

And to 'be troubled' means to be 'violently agitated,' or 'angered.'

All the merchants who had been benefactors of Tyre's trading system would then blame Tyre for their own downfall.

"The merchants among the peoples will hiss (whistle of scorn) at you..." Ezekiel 27:36 NKJV

And once again, God proclaims that Tyre's fall will be forever.

"You will become a horror (terror), and be no more forever." Ezekiel 27:36 NKJV

Thus, the great commercial center in the east was devastated because of pride and her attitude towards Israel.

Looking backward to the future

God spoke to Ezekiel during the early years of Judah's deportation to Babylon. There is as much revealed in Scripture about Tyre's judgment as there is about Babylon's judgment. Their roles in history differ greatly; however, they both provide explicit examples of the future.

While researching some history of Tyre, the following quote from a learned historian caught my eye.

"The Bible contains a number of specific prophesies concerning Tyre. Many of these prophecies have been used by apologists in defense of the divine origin of Scripture because their fulfillment was very accurate. It is therefore worth examining each in some detail."

In the prophecy that God gave to Ezekiel, the focus changed from the city of Tyre to the king of Tyre. The king of Tyre at the time Ezekiel prophesied was Ittobaal II; however, the discourse is not limited to this single king. The motives of many of Tyre's kings since the time of David and Solomon were consistent.

The king of Tyre claimed to be deity

God told Ezekiel to tell the king of Tyre the following:

"Because your heart is lifted up, and you say, 'I am a god, I sit in the seat of gods, in the midst of the seas,' yet you are a man, and not a god...'" Ezekiel 28:2 NKJV

Ezekiel told the king that his heart was haughty and proud.

The king of Tyre thought he was a god by using the word *Elohim* which suggests a divine connection. When God said that he was not a god, the word *El* was used which connotes 'a pagan god,' or 'a man.'

God chided the king because the king thought he was wiser than Daniel. God revealed that the king was wise, but not in the same way, or for the same purpose.

"By your wisdom and understanding you have acquired riches for yourself, and have acquired gold and silver for your treasuries. By your great wisdom, by your trade you have increased your riches, and your heart is lifted up because of your riches..." Ezekiel 28:4-5 NASB

What a difference between the king's wisdom and that of Daniel. While God used Daniel to reveal His kingdom, the king of Tyre relentlessly pursued riches and wealth for himself. The result was that he became very proud.

God was about to speak again. He revealed that He was about to bring a foreign nation against the king of Tyre. God described the nation as the most terrible of the nations.

And they will draw their swords against the beauty of your wisdom and defile (profane) your splendor.
Ezekiel 28:7b NASB

The result would be that the king would be thrown down into the pit of death, destruction, and decay.

"Will you still say before him who slays you, 'I am a god'? But you shall be a man, and not a god, in the hand of him who slays you." Ezekiel 28:9 NKJV

Again, the king would use *Elohim* while God uses *El*.

The king would die the death of the uncircumcised, one who is morally and spiritually unclean, by the hand of strangers.

The king of Tyre imitated his father, the devil

God said that Tyre believed they lacked for nothing.

"O Tyre, you have said, 'I am perfect in beauty.'" Ezekiel 27:3 NASB

The word 'Perfect' in the present context means 'complete.'

And then God tells Ezekiel to take up a lamentation against the king of Tyre by comparing his heart to that of the devil himself.

God speaks of the devil.

"You were the seal of perfection, full of wisdom and perfect in beauty. You were in Eden, the garden of God...You

were the anointed cherub who covers; I established you...You were perfect in your ways from the day you were created, till iniquity was found in you." Ezekiel 28:12-15 NKJV

As a created celestial being, the devil was the sum of perfection, or complete. He was full of wisdom and appointed to be the one to defend God. The devil was perfect in all ways from the time of his creation, until iniquity (perverseness, unrighteousness, unjustness, and wickedness) was found in him.

Then God speaks of the king of Tyre and compares his heart to that of the devil.

"By the abundance of your trade you were internally filled with violence (cruelty, wickedness), and you sinned." Ezekiel 28:16 NASB

Notice the similarity, 'until iniquity was found in you,' and 'you sinned.' They both had a choice, and both made the wrong choice.

But notice the cause of the king of Tyre's sin, 'by the abundance of your trade' brought on his sin. Materialism and the desire to increase wealth defiled his heart and mind.

"Your heart was lifted up because of your beauty; you corrupted your wisdom by reason of your splendor. I cast you to the ground; I put you before kings, that they may see you." Ezekiel 28:17 NASB

The king became haughty and proud due to his success in trading. He misused his wisdom for selfish reasons and ungodly priorities. God would bring him down and lay him before kings as an example of such folly.

"By the multitude of your iniquities, in the unrighteousness of your trade, you profaned your sanctuaries."
Ezekiel 28:18 NASB

The king had defiled his sanctuaries, the consecrated places that he had established by the wickedness of his trading.

Then God reiterated that he would spill the king's 'ashes upon the earth in the sight of all who saw you.' Again, the king was an example for all who saw him and knew what he stood for.

The ending words are the same as the ending of the other two times that God spoke to Ezekiel on the matter of Tyre and her kings.

"All who knew you among the peoples are astonished at you; you have become a horror, and shall be no more forever." Ezekiel 28:19 NKJV

The significance of Tyre in the Day of the LORD

Just prior to the return of Christ to end Daniel's 70th week, the identification of the great harlot and her representative city will be revealed. The prophets of old spoke much about the harlot and her city 2,500 years before Christ.

There were two ancient cities in the Old Testament representing the city of the future; Tyre and Babylon. The deranged city of the future will be called Babylon.

And significantly, Ezekiel revealed the motives of the trading partners along with their fate. Ezekiel's prophecy had both short-term and long-term applications.

The short-term application was fulfilled in the ancient city of Tyre, while the long-term application will be fulfilled in the rebuilt city of Babylon, as described in Revelation 18.

Therefore, while Ezekiel told of the long-term application of his prophecy, that prophecy is presently a short-term prophecy for the current generation.

The world needs to take heed and read the leaves on the fig tree.

Recall the final verse in Revelation 17.

"And the woman whom you saw is that great city, which reigns over the kings of the earth." Revelation 17:18 NASB

That great city represents both an idolatrous system and a central physical headquarters for that system. The great harlot will have committed fornication with all the kings of the earth. Her harlotry became the standard, or norm, for all nations.

The lament over the demise of the future capital mercantile city

"The kings of the earth who committed fornication and lived luxuriously with her will weep and lament for her, when they see the smoke of her burning..." Revelation 18:9 NASB

Recall that Tyre's merchants of old also wept and lamented over her fall.

"Then all the princes of the sea will come down from their thrones...and they will take up a lament for you... 'How you have perished...O renowned city...All who handle the oars, the mariners, all the pilots of the sea will come down from their ships...and weep for you...in their wailing for you they will take up a lamentation...what city is like Tyre...?'" Ezekiel 26:16-17, 27:29, 31-32 NKJV

John heard a voice from heaven telling of the loss of business due to the future city's fall.

"And the merchants of the earth will weep and mourn over her; for no one buys their merchandise anymore." Revelation 18:11 NKJV

The voice then listed the products that would no longer be traded. The list is very similar to the list of merchandise traded by ancient Tyre.

- Gold and silver

- Precious (valued, expensive, prized, esteemed) stones and pearls

- Fine linen and purple, silk and scarlet

- Every kind of citron wood

- Every kind of object of ivory

- Every kind of object of most precious wood, bronze, iron, and marble

- Cinnamon and incense

- Fragrant oil and frankincense

- Wine and oil

- Fine flour and wheat

- Cattle and sheep

- Horses and chariots

- Bodies and souls of men

Recall the voice from heaven revealed that the kings of the earth had lived luxuriously with the great 'city.' While the NKJV uses the word 'luxury,' the KJV instead uses the words 'delicacy' or 'deliciously' which are derived from 'wantonness.'

Numerous synonyms for the Greek 'wantonness' include 'abundance,' 'pleasure,' 'sensuous,' 'self gratification,' 'indulgence,' 'never enough,' or to 'abandon reins of religion or reason.'

Interestingly, contemporary definitions by Webster for 'wantonness' include 'lavish,' 'undisciplined,' 'limitless,' and 'lustful.'

The future mercantile capital city itself is described with similar adjectives.

"... 'Alas, alas; that great city that was clothed in fine linen, purple, and scarlet, and adorned with gold and precious stones and pearls! For in one hour such great riches came to nothing.'" Revelation 18:16-17 NKJV

The 'great city' dealt more with items of luxury than of necessity.

"The fruit that your soul longed for has gone from you, and all the things which are rich and splendid have gone from you, and you shall find them no more at all The merchants of these things, who became rich by her, will stand at a distance...weeping and wailing..." Revelation 18:14-15 NKJV

Not only did the merchants who traded with the mercantile city weep and mourn over her demise, so did all others who made their livelihood from the city's activities.

"Every shipmaster, all who travel by ship, sailors, and as many as trade on the sea...cried out when they saw the smoke of her burning...They threw dust on their heads and cried out, weeping and wailing, and saying, 'Alas, alas,...for in one hour she is made desolate.'" Revelation 18:17-19 NKJV

Human slavery was involved in ancient Tyre as well as listed in the future mercantile city's activities. Even today human sex trafficking is a multi-billion dollar industry in the United States.

Tyre represents key components of Babylon, past and future

The city of Tyre presented a picture of the ancient city of Babel. The future city will be called Babylon which is, according to the prophet Zechariah, to be built at the same location as ancient Babel.

At this point we'll focus on the prophesied destruction of the city along with accompanying ramifications introduced by Ezekiel.

To illustrate the magnificence of the parallelism in Scripture, we'll examine several individual verses in Revelation and compare those verses with prophecies spoken more than two millennia ago.

For example, the following verse describes the permanent destruction of the rebuilt city of Babylon.

"...Babylon the great is fallen, is fallen, and has become a dwelling place of demons, a prison for every foul spirit, and a cage for every unclean and hated bird!"
Revelation 18:2 NKJV

Then consider the following from Ezekiel as he describes the destruction of ancient Tyre.

For thus says the Lord GOD, "When I shall make you a desolate city, like the cities which are not inhabited, when I shall bring up the deep over you, and the great waters will cover you..." Ezekiel 26:19 NASB

Then John describes the great harlot's methodology and spiritual adultery.

"For all the nations have drunk of the wine of the wrath of her fornication, the kings of the earth have committed fornication with her, and the merchants of the earth have become rich through the abundance of her luxury." Revelation 18:3 NKJV

As per Jeremiah:

For thus the LORD, the God of Israel... "Take this cup of the wine of wrath from My hand, and cause all the nations...to drink it." Jeremiah 25:15 NKJV

Babylon has been a golden cup in the hand of the LORD, intoxicating all the earth. The nations have drunk of her wine; therefore the nations are going mad. Jeremiah 51:7 NASB

"Damascus was your merchant because of the abundance of goods you made, because of your many luxury items..." Ezekiel 27:18 NKJV

At the end of days another angel cries out from heaven...

"...Come out of her, my people, lest you share in her sins, and lest you receive of her plagues." Revelation 18:4 NKJV

The same warning 2,500 years ago:

"Flee from the midst of Babylon, and every one save his life! Do not be cut off in her iniquity, for this is the time of the LORD's vengeance...for her judgment reaches to heaven and is lifted up to the skies." Jeremiah 51:6, 9b NKJV

The angel continues:

"To the degree that she glorified herself and lived sensuously (luxuriously), to the same degree give her torment and mourning, for she says in her heart, 'I sit as a queen and I am not a widow, and will never see mourning (sorrow).'" Revelation 18:7 NASB

Ezekiel spoke of the haughtiness and pride of Tyre.

"Thus says the Lord God: 'Because your heart is lifted up, and you say, "I am a god, I sit in the seat of gods..." yet you are a man, and not a god, though you set your heart as the heart of a god.' Your heart was lifted up because of your beauty; you corrupted your wisdom for the sake of your splendor." Ezekiel 28:2, 17a NKJV

And Isaiah spoke more than a century before Ezekiel referencing Babylon, the capital city of Babylonia, while unknowingly describing the future city.

"And you say, 'I shall be a lady forever,'...Therefore hear this now, you who are given to pleasures, who dwell securely who say in your heart, 'I am, and there is no one else besides me; I shall not sit as a widow, nor shall I know the loss of children.'" Isaiah 47:7-8 NKJV

Then the angel will speak again in the end of days, revealing the judgment of the great harlot.

"For this reason in one day her plagues will come, pestilence (death) and mourning and famine, and she will be burned up with fire..." Revelation 18:8 NASB

Ezekiel's forewarning of Tyre's burning due to her iniquity of trading:

"...Therefore I have brought fire from the midst of you; it has consumed you, and I have turned you to ashes on the earth..." Ezekiel 28:18 NASB

The angel announces that mighty Babylon would also be destroyed with great violence never to rise again.

And a strong angel took up a stone like a great millstone and threw it into the sea, saying, "Thus will Babylon, the great city, be thrown down with violence, and will not be found any longer." Revelation 18:21 NASB

Recall how God described Babylon's fall 600 years before the birth of Christ.

"...Just so shall Babylon sink down and not rise again, because of the calamity that I am going to bring upon her..." Jeremiah 51:64 NASB

And at the end of each of the three chapters in Ezekiel that describes Tyre's judgment, the word states that her fall is permanent.

"I shall bring terrors on you, and you will be no more; though you will be sought, you will never be found again," says the Lord God. Ezekiel 26:21 NASB

The angel expounds on Babylon's fall by confirming that there will be no more pleasant music heard in her.

"And the sound of harpists and musicians and flute players and trumpeters will not be heard in you any longer..." Revelation 18:22 NASB

The same words were spoken by Ezekiel.

"So I will silence the sound of your songs, and the sound of your harps will be heard no more." Ezekiel 26:14 NASB

And the causes of Babylon's fall? The great harlot deceived the leaders of all the nations.

"...for your merchants were the great men of the earth, because all the nations were deceived by your sorcery." Revelation 18:23 NASB

The substance of the great harlot's deceit centered on convincing each nation that its greatness, or success, was measured by its wealth.

In addition, the great harlot appealed to, and satisfied, the desires of the natural man.

Chapter 9

The Rise and fall of Mighty Babylon

The Bible has much to say about 'Babylon.' For example, why and how did she achieve greatness, why and how did she fall in the past, and why and how will she fall again in the near future.

Babylon's ideology has and does affect all the nations on earth.

"For all the nations have drunk of the wine of the wrath of her fornication, the kings of the earth have committed fornication with her, and the merchants of the earth have become rich through the abundance of her luxury." Revelation 18:3 NKJV

Only the naïve would think that America is excluded.

When prophets spoke of Babylon, there was typically both short-term and long-term implications. Plus, seeing that Babylon universally represents that which God detests, the words of the prophets should be taken to heart by all nations, especially God's chosen nation of Israel.

And recall how Paul explained that Israel's lessons in the past apply to us today.

Now these things happened to them (Israel) as an example, and they were written for our instruction, upon whom the ends of the ages have come. Therefore let him who thinks he stands take heed lest he fall.
1 Corinthians 10:11-12 NASB

Therefore; let's begin with the Old Testament prophets.

Habakkuk revealed God's denunciation of ancient Babylon

God pronounced five 'woes' against Babylon for their haughtiness and despicable agenda.

"...Woe (alas) to him who increases what is not his – and makes himself rich with loans?" Habakkuk 2:6 NASB

God warned that there would be consequences for Babylon's actions which included assessing excessive taxation on their conquered nations.

Babylon is told that through God's sovereign power, the nations whom they have conquered would repay on the appointed day.

"Because you have looted (plundered) many nations, all the remainder of the peoples will loot you – because

of human bloodshed and violence done to the land..."
Habakkuk 2:8 NASB

Not only was Babylon exercising power over the nations whom they had plundered, they did so with violence and bloodshed. God would shortly turn the tables on Babylon and the remnant of the plundered nations would take spoil from their plunderers.

"Woe to him who gets (covets) evil gain for his house to put his nest on high..." Habakkuk 2:9 NASB

Plundering begins with coveting. Babylon sought to gain wealth so as to appear rich to those nations around them. They also gained confidence and thought they would not see disaster.

"Woe to him who builds a city with bloodshed and founds a town with violence!? Habakkuk 2:12 NASB

Babylon's expansion was gained by bloodshed and violence.

"Woe to you who make your neighbors drink, who mix in your venom even to make them drunk..."
Habakkuk 2:15 NASB

'Drunk' is used figuratively to represent Babylon's attempts to make their conquered nations feel humble by suppressing independence.

Once again, the tables would be turned upside down by Almighty God.

"You will be filled with disgrace rather than honor...The cup on the LORD's right hand will come around to you, and utter disgrace will come upon your glory." Habakkuk 2:16 NASB

God reminded Babylon that their despicable actions included violence and bloodshed. But such actions will be returned to them in like manner.

God taunts Babylon for their love and respect for idols made with hands. Even if they were overlaid with gold and silver, 'yet in it (them) there is no breath at all.'

"Woe to him who says to a piece of wood, 'Awake!' To a dumb stone, 'Arise!' Habakkuk 2:19 NASB

Babylon's King Nebuchadnezzar had been prepared to fulfill God's plan

Recall Nebuchadnezzar's dream which only the prophet Daniel could interpret. Daniel began by explaining the head of gold on Nebuchadnezzar's metallic vision.

"You, O king, are the king of kings, to whom the God of heaven has given the kingdom, the power, the strength, and the glory; and wherever the sons of men dwell...He has given them into your hand and has caused you to rule over them all. You are the head of gold." Daniel 2:37-38 NASB

Everything that the king of Babylon had was given to him by God to fulfill His purpose.

Consider the words of God given to Jeremiah.

"I have made the earth, the men and the beasts which are on the face of the earth...and I will give it to the one who is pleasing in My sight. And now I have given all these lands into the hand of Nebuchadnezzar king of Babylon, My servant..." Jeremiah 27:5-6 NASB

God confirms His omniscience through not only His creation, but the fulfillment of His purpose. In this case God appointed the king of Babylon, whom He called His servant, to rule over the nations - temporarily.

God also told of the consequences to any nation that didn't obey His command to submit to Babylon's king.

"And it will be, that the nation or the kingdom which will not serve him, Nebuchadnezzar king of Babylon, and which will not put its neck under the yoke of the king of Babylon, I will punish that nation with the sword, with famine, and with pestilence..." Jeremiah 27:8 NASB

Babylon's sin of idolatry

Recall Habakkuk's fifth woe.

"Woe to him who says to a piece of wood, 'Awake!' To a dumb stone, 'Arise!' Habakkuk 2:19 NASB

However; Babylon was very active with idols.

All mankind is stupid, devoid of knowledge; every goldsmith is put to shame by his idols, for his molten images are deceitful, and there is no breath in them.
Jeremiah 51:17-18 NASB

Heaven and earth will celebrate over the destruction of Babylon's idols, both short-term and long-term.

"Therefore behold, days are coming when I shall punish the idols of Babylon; and her whole land will be put to shame, and all her slain will fall in her midst. Then heaven and earth and all that is in them will shout for joy over Babylon, for the destroyers will come to her...declares the LORD." Jeremiah 51:47-48 NASB

God condemned Babylon for her idols and images.

Babylon's sin of pride

"Summon many against Babylon...Repay her according to her work; for she has become arrogant against the LORD, against the Holy One of Israel." Jeremiah 50:29 NASB

All who are proud against God will be humbled in His timing.

Then Isaiah tells how the occupants of hell will scoff at Babylon's king.

"Hell (Sheol) from beneath is excited about you, to meet you at your coming...all the kings of the nations...shall speak and say to you: 'Have you also become as weak as we? Have you become like us? Your pomp is brought down to Sheol...'" Isaiah 14:9-11 NKJV

'Pomp' is the same as pride and arrogance. Jeremiah went on to say that Babylon's arrogance was in fact a major cause of her fall.

"Behold, I am against you, O arrogant one...for your day has come, the time when I shall punish you. And the arrogant one will stumble and fall with no one to raise him up..." Jeremiah 50:31-32 NASB

Babylon's sin of mistreating God's people

Thus says the LORD of hosts, "The sons of Israel are oppressed, and the sons of Judah as well; and all who took them captive have held them fast, they have refused to let them go." Jeremiah 50:33 NASB

The Babylonians had likewise scoffed at Israel when God chastised His own.

"Because you were glad, because you rejoiced, you destroyers of My heritage...because of the wrath of the LORD she (Babylon) shall not be inhabited, but she shall be wholly desolate. Everyone who goes by Babylon shall

be horrified...For it is the vengeance of the LORD...as she has done, so do to her..." Jeremiah 50:11a, 13, 15b NKJV

So many times in the Bible, God tells of His wrath and required vengeance on His enemies because of His very righteousness.

Israel's capital city of Jerusalem wailed over her mistreatment by Babylon.

"Nebuchadnezzar king of Babylon has devoured me and crushed me...He has swallowed me like a monster...He has washed me away (spit me out). May the violence done to me and to my flesh be upon Babylon..." Jeremiah 51:34-35 NASB

God responds to Jerusalem's woes.

"Therefore thus says the LORD, 'Behold, I am going to plead your case and exact full vengeance for you...and Babylon will become a heap of ruins...an object of horror and hissing, without inhabitants...'"
Jeremiah 51:36-37 NASB

Babylon was naïve enough to think they were serving God by plundering His people because they had been disobedient.

"...And their adversaries have said, 'We are not guilty, inasmuch as they have sinned against the LORD who is the habitation of righteousness, even the LORD, the hope of their fathers.'" Jeremiah 50:7 NASB

Babylon's judgment was imminent.

Therefore hear the plan of the LORD which He has planned against Babylon, and His purposes which He has purposed against the land of the Chaldeans...At the shout, "Babylon has been seized!" the earth is shaken, and an outcry is heard among the nations. Jeremiah 50:45-46 NASB

All the actions against Babylon are in accordance with God's plan and purpose which He determined before the foundation of the world.

Babylon's successor is revealed

The LORD has aroused the spirit of the kings of the Medes, because His purpose is against Babylon to destroy it; for it is the vengeance of the LORD... Jeremiah 51:11 NASB

Isaiah wrote a century before Jeremiah and previously announced who would replace Babylon as the world's power.

Behold, I am going to stir up the Medes against them... and Babylon, the beauty of kingdoms...will be as when God overthrew Sodom and Gomorrah. It will never be inhabited or lived in from generation to generation; nor will the Arab pitch his tent there... Isaiah 13:17, 19-20 NASB

Babylon would be overrun by the Medes and Persians in the short-run.

*"You are My war-club, My weapon of war; and with
you I shatter nations, and with you I destroy kingdoms...
and with you I shatter governors and prefects (rulers)."*
Jeremiah 51:20, 23b NASB

Babylon is warned to prepare for the attack by the king
of the Medes.

*"And the land will tremble and sorrow; for every
purpose of the LORD shall be performed against Babylon,
to make the land of Babylon desolation without inhabitant."*
Jeremiah 51:29 NKJV

It is always so powerful to see that every purpose of God
will be performed as He promised. Why would any nation
turn against almighty God?

*"'For I will rise up against them,' says the LORD of
hosts, 'and cut off from Babylon the name and remnant, and
offspring and posterity,' says the LORD."* Isaiah 14:22 NKJV

Now let's see what Jeremiah had to say shortly before
King Cyrus of the Medes took Babylon and freed the Jewish
captives in 539 BC, as previously announced by Isaiah 140
years before Cyrus was even born.

*The word which the LORD spoke concerning Babylon...
through Jeremiah the prophet: "Declare and proclaim
among the nations...Her images have been put to shame,
her idols have been shattered. For a nation has come up*

against her out of the north; it will make her land an object of horror..." Jeremiah 50:1-3 NASB

God condemned Babylon for her idolatry, her pride, her mistreatment of His people and the shedding of innocent blood.

The king of Tyre and the king of Babylon had much in common

Just like Ezekiel illustrated that the king of Tyre possessed the attributes of the devil himself, Isaiah uses the same methodology to define the king of Babylon.

Isaiah begins by stating that Lucifer was cast out of heaven because of pride.

"For you have said in your heart: 'I will ascend into heaven, I will exalt my throne above the stars of God...I will ascend above the heights of the clouds, I will be like the Most High.'" Isaiah 14:13-14 NKJV

'Exalt' is very similar to the above 'pomp' and carries the meaning of being haughty, presumptuous, and/or proud.

Only God has the authority to say, "I will," and the power to make happen what He says He will do.

And God's response to Lucifer's pride?

"Nevertheless you will be thrust down to Sheol, to the recesses of the pit (dungeon)." Isaiah 14:15 NASB

Those witnessing the arrival of the proud king are in near unbelief.

"Those who see you will gaze at you, they will ponder over you, saying, 'Is this the man who made the earth tremble, who shook kingdoms, who made the world like a wilderness and overthrew its cities, who did not allow his prisoners to go home?'" Isaiah 14:16-17 NASB

The kings of the world are amazed to see the end of one who appeared to be indestructible, who destroyed cities and people, who wouldn't release his prisoners.

Babylon had reached the point where there was no remedy

Then God prepares for the short-term destruction of Babylon; their king and all the people. And in the latter days Babylon and those who were made drunk with her harlotry will also be destroyed and never rise again.

God then explains that He had used Babylon as a tool to perform His plan.

"How the hammer of the whole earth has been cut off and broken! How Babylon has become an object of horror among the nations! I set a snare for you, and you were also

caught, O Babylon, while you yourself were not aware..."
Jeremiah 50:23-24 NASB

The nations do not realize that their actions reflect what God has put into their hearts to perform His will. At the time in history reported by Jeremiah, Babylon was the pre-ordained kingdom God used to suppress both Egypt and Assyria.

"The LORD has opened His armory and has brought forth the weapons of His indignation, for it is a work of the Lord GOD of hosts in the land of the Chaldeans."
Jeremiah 50:25 NASB

God's weapons of indignation are the weapons He uses to execute His wrath against those who despise His word and oppress His people.

Why Babylon had to go

After telling His people again to flee from the midst of Babylon, because it is the time for God's vengeance, Jeremiah reveals more about God's strategy and Babylon's degradation.

Babylon has been a golden cup in the hand of the LORD, intoxicating all the earth. The nations have drunk of her wine; therefore the nations are going mad. Jeremiah 51:7 NASB

Note the sovereignty of God. He held the golden cup and made all the nations drink of it, resulting in their being drunk and deranged.

For the LORD has both purposed and performed what He spoke concerning the inhabitants of Babylon. Jeremiah 51:12b NASB

No matter how powerful Babylon thought she was, she was no match for Almighty God.

"Though Babylon should ascend to the heavens, and though she should fortify her lofty stronghold, from Me destroyers will come to her," declares the LORD... "For the LORD is going to destroy Babylon, and He will make her loud noise vanish from her..." Jeremiah 51:53, 55 NASB

The sum of the matter is that no power in the universe could prevent God from executing His justice on Babylon.

For the LORD is a God of recompense, He will fully repay. "And I shall make her princes and her wise men drunk, her governors, her prefects, and her mighty men, that they may sleep a perpetual sleep and not wake up," declares the King, whose name is the LORD of hosts. Jeremiah 51:56b-57 NASB

One can only wonder in awe of the sovereignty of Almighty God, His purpose, and His foreordained detailed plan of execution.

All nations better take heed to see if any of their ways coincide with those of Babylon. And keep in mind that all nations will be raised up and brought down per the immutable plan of God established before the foundation of the world.

Drunk with the blood of the saints...

We've seen that the 'Mother of Harlots...' was the source of idolatry and fornication (spiritual adultery) as revealed in Revelation 17 and 18.

However, equally significant is the fact that she is also the source of the shed blood of God's people.

And I saw the woman drunk with the blood of the saints, and with the blood of the witnesses of Jesus.
Revelation 17:6 NASB

To be drunk means to have an insatiable desire for something, and never have enough.

To be a saint or a witness or martyr of Jesus means to be guiltless, blameless, or innocent. It definitely means that one is not worthy of death.

During the 'Day of the LORD,' much is said about the killing of innocents.

A major sin of Babylon - past, present, and future - was the killing of God's people.

"And in her was found the blood of prophets and of saints and of all who have been slain on the earth." Revelation 18:24 NASB

Immediately after the fall of the future city, there is great celebration in heaven.

"...Alleluia! Salvation and glory and honor and power belong to the Lord our God! For true and righteous are His judgments, because He has judged the great harlot who corrupted the earth with her fornication; and He has avenged on her the blood of His servants shed by her." Revelation 19:1-2 NKJV

Earlier, during the great tribulation when an angel poured the third bowl judgment on the earth, which turned the oceans to blood, the angel revealed the reason for the blood judgment.

"...for they poured out (shed) the blood of saints and prophets, and Thou hast given them blood to drink. They deserve it." Revelation 16:6 NASB

The Bible had revealed that the price for shedding innocent blood was the blood of the offender. All of God's judgments are righteous and just.

Martyrs during the tribulation were waiting for God's judgment and vengeance for their killers.

When Christ opened the fifth seal, John saw and heard the cry of the martyrs.

And when He broke the fifth seal, I saw underneath the altar the souls of those who had been slain because of the word of God, and because of the testimony which they had maintained; and they cried out with a loud voice, saying, "How long, O Lord, holy and true, wilt Thou refrain from judging and avenging our blood on those who dwell on the earth?" Revelation 6:9-10 NASB

They were told to rest for a little while longer until their brethren, who were also ordained to be killed for the word of God, joined them.

The judgment for taking the life of another, with malice or purpose, was addressed by God in ages past. At that time He revealed the reason for His required judgment.

"Whoever sheds man's blood, by man his blood shall be shed, for in the image of God He made man..." Genesis 9:6 NASB

Man is the only of God's creations made in His own image. The righteous judgment for maliciously killing a man, therefore, is to pay for that sin with the offender's own life. God said that the murderer's blood must be shed at the hands of others. That is the original definition of 'capital punishment.'

God's word has never changed, nor has capital punishment ever been annulled.

Shortly after the Exodus from Egypt, God revealed His law, i.e. standard of His righteousness, to His chosen nation.

The 6th of the 10 Commandments was simply:

"You shall not murder (kill). Exodus 20:13 NASB

God reiterated His holy law and explained the sanctity of the blood.

"...for it (blood) is the life of all flesh. Its blood sustains life...for the life of all flesh is its blood..." Leviticus 17:14 NKJV

God then explained that the only way to atone for the sin of shedding blood was to repay with the blood of the one who shed it.

The killing of innocents through the ages

According to the Bible, the worst offenders of killing innocents were the Israelites themselves; the very ones that were given the oracles of God.

King David acknowledged his participation in such activities, but He pleaded for God to forgive him. Perhaps David was referring to Bathsheba's husband Uriah, inasmuch as the 51st Psalm was written after David's adulterous affair.

"Have mercy upon me, O God...Create in me a clean heart, O God...Restore to me the joy of Your salvation... Deliver me from the guilt of bloodshed, O God..."
Psalm 51:1a, 10a, 12a, 14a NKJV

In later years of his kingship, David wrote another wonderful Psalm about the absolute sovereignty of his God.

David acknowledged that God knew him before his birth.

My frame (bones) was not hidden from Thee, when I was made in secret, and skillfully wrought in the depths of the earth (my mother's womb). Thine eyes have seen my unformed substance; and in Thy book they were all written, the days that were ordained for me, when as yet there was not one of them. Psalm 139:15-16 NASB

Thus David acknowledged that God knew him and fashioned his days before he was ever born. God saw David's life while he was still in his mother's womb.

Therefore, a child in the womb is one of the 'innocent.' Progressivism doesn't quite define life in that manner.

Another Psalmist spoke of innocent children being slaughtered by Israelite parents.

They even sacrificed their sons and their daughters to the demons, and shed innocent blood, the blood of their

sons and their daughters, whom they sacrificed to the idols of Canaan; and the land was polluted with the blood. Psalm 106:37-38 NASB

The Israelites offered their newborn sons and daughters to the Canaanite god Molech.

Ezekiel reported the same hideous acts of idolatry.

"Moreover, you took your sons and daughters whom you had borne to Me, and you sacrificed them to idols to be devoured. Were your harlotries so small a matter? You slaughtered My children, and offered them up to idols by causing them to pass through the fire." Ezekiel 16:20-21 NASB

Israel's consequence?

"You have become guilty by the blood which you have shed, and defiled by your idols which you have made. Thus you have brought your day near and have come to your years..." Ezekiel 22:4 NASB

Israel's days were numbered because they offered up their children to idols that they had made with their own hands.

David's son Solomon also addressed the shedding of blood of innocents.

There are six things which the LORD hates, yes, seven which are an abomination to Him: haughty eyes,

a lying tongue, and hands that shed innocent blood...
Proverbs 6:16-17 NASB

Such acts were considered an abomination before God; and remember the great harlot is the 'mother of...the abominations of the earth' who was drunk with the blood of the saints...

The detestable sin was found in Jerusalem and accepted by Israel's kings.

Moreover, Manasseh shed very much innocent blood until he had filled Jerusalem from one end to another...
2 Kings 21:16 NASB

Such sins caused God to bring Nebuchadnezzar to plunder Jerusalem.

Surely at the command of the LORD it came upon Judah... and also for the innocent blood which he (Manasseh) shed...
2 Kings 24:3-4 NASB

In the early chapters of Isaiah as he was describing the wickedness of Judah, he likewise spoke of the shedding of blood.

"So when you spread out our hands in prayer, I will hide My eyes from you, Yes, even though you multiply prayers, I will not listen. Your hands are full of bloodshed."
Isaiah 1:15 NASB

But Israel did not change their ways; because at the end of Isaiah's writings, Israel's sin is mentioned again.

But your iniquities have made a separation between you and your God, and your sins have hid His face from you... for your hands are defiled with blood... Isaiah 59:2-3 NASB

In the early chapters of Jeremiah, he speaks of God's case against Israel which includes shedding blood of innocents.

"Also on your skirts is found the blood of the lives of the poor innocents. I have not found it by secret search, but plainly on all these things. Yet you say, 'because I am innocent...'" Jeremiah 2:34-35 NKJV

God subsequently states that if Israel would repent of such sins, He would let them dwell safely in their land.

"For if you truly amend your ways and your deeds, if you truly practice justice between a man and his neighbor... and do not shed innocent blood in this place...then I will let you dwell in this place, in the land that I gave to your fathers forever and ever." Jeremiah 7:5-7 NASB

But repentance didn't follow, so then God declares that He will bring catastrophe on the land.

The Israelites were blatantly involved in the sin of killing innocents, yet did not acknowledge it as sin.

The Pharisees also had blood of innocents on their hands

Let's examine what was perhaps Jesus' harshest denunciation of the Pharisees.

The Pharisees had just told Jesus that if they had lived in the days of their fathers, they would have honored the prophets.

"...If we had been living in the days of our fathers, we would not have been partners with them in shedding the blood of the prophets." Matthew 23:30 NASB

Jesus called them hypocrites, serpents, and brood of vipers. He then told them what they would do to His messengers in the future.

"Consequently you bear witness against yourselves, that you are sons of those who murdered the prophets. Fill up then the measure of the guilt of your fathers...how shall you escape the sentence of hell? Therefore, behold, I am sending you prophets and wise men and scribes; some of them you will kill and crucify, and some of them you will scourge in your synagogues, and persecute from city to city, that upon you may fall the guilt of all the righteous blood shed on earth...Truly I say to you, all these things shall come upon this generation." Matthew 23:31-36 NASB

Looking forward to the 'Day of the Lord'

Recall, future Babylon is called the great harlot in the end of days, and her everlasting destruction is described in the book of Revelation.

Remember these two verses that describe the future Babylon.

"For all the nations have drunk of the wine of the wrath of her fornication, the kings of the earth have committed fornication with her and the merchants of the earth have become rich through the abundance of her luxury." Revelation 18:3 NKJV

And I saw the woman drunk with the blood of the saints, and with the blood of the witnesses of Jesus. Revelation 17:6 NASB

Has America emulated Babylon and lowered herself to harlotry?

Several Biblical passages can be examined to answer that question. Let's begin with a passage penned nearly 3,500 years ago. The lesson is to remember the LORD for it is He who provides all things.

"Beware lest you forget the LORD your God by not keeping His commandments and His ordinances and His statutes which I am commanding you today; lest, when you have eaten and are satisfied, and have built good houses and lived in them, and when your herds and your flocks multiply, and your silver and gold multiply...then your heart becomes proud, and you forget the LORD your God who brought you out...of the house of slavery." Deuteronomy 8:11-14 NASB

The major point is that God would provide Israel all she could ever dream of having. When the promises came to fruition in their new land, they were not to forget the source of their prosperity and blessings.

They were neither to boast nor take credit for anything God had provided.

"Otherwise, you may say in your heart, 'My power and the strength of my hand made me this wealth.'" Deuteronomy 8:17 NASB

Approximately 800 years later, after a history of disobedience, God recounted Israel's required judgment. Both northern Israel and southern Judah were labeled as harlots because they had committed spiritual adultery against their betrothed.

"Therefore, thus says the Lord God, 'Because you have forgotten Me and cast Me behind your back, bear now the punishment of your lewdness and your harlotries.'" Ezekiel 23:35 NASB

Recall, the Hebrew for 'forgotten' means 'to be oblivious to because of lack of attention,' i.e. a conscious forsaking.

The word 'lewdness' means 'evil' or 'wicked,' while 'cast' means 'to consciously put someone or something away.'

And the word 'harlotry' or 'whoredom' means metaphorically spiritual adultery and/or idolatry. It also carries the meaning of illegal contact between Israel and other nations. To depend on other nations or coalitions for their safety instead of God was considered to be harlotry.

Harlotry is mentioned throughout the Bible and is summarized in the Book of Revelation where Babylon is called:

"Mystery, Babylon the Great, the mother of harlots and of the abominations of the earth." Revelation 17:5 NKJV

The Bible reveals that the final ten nation confederation (coalition) under the rule of the seventh and final world kingdom will destroy the great harlot.

"And the ten horns which you saw, and the beast, these will hate the harlot and will make her desolate and naked, and will eat her flesh and will burn her up with fire." Revelation 17:16 NASB

Several questions to consider:

- Has America also forsaken her God and committed spiritual adultery by placing their faith and trust in materialism?

- Is America more concerned with transitory things than eternal things?

- Does America's value system focus on the 'here and now?'

- Does America have the blood of innocents on their hands?

If the answer to any of the above questions is 'yes,' then America has been deceived and been led down the path to harlotry. However, she is not alone.

Remember the following key verse.

"For all the nations have drunk of the wine of the wrath of her fornication, the kings of the earth have committed fornication with her, and the merchants of the earth have become rich through the abundance of her luxury." Revelation 18:3 NKJV

The second word in the above passage is 'all.'

There is much comfort in knowing that a person is not 'saved' based on the performance of the nation in which he/she is a citizen. A person is saved with a one-on-one relationship with the Lamb of God. The company of such in this present age is called the 'church.'

And while many individual people will repent, no nation other than Israel is promised eternal existence as a nation.

Chapter 10

History is Repeating Itself

After God created the birds to fly above the earth, fish to fill the waters of the seas, and every living thing that moves upon the earth, He created man in His own image.

God's first command to His newest and highest creation was then revealed.

And God blessed them; and God said to them, "Be fruitful and multiply, and fill the earth, and subdue it; and rule over the fish of the sea and over the birds of the sky, and over every living that that moves on the earth."
Genesis 1:28 NASB

'Subdue' means to bring under submission, while 'rule' means to have 'dominion over,' or 'reign.'

Soon thereafter deceit and disobedience took place in the garden.

Man's continued disobedience led to judgment

The earth and its caretakers would have been utterly destroyed had it not been for a righteous man named Noah.

Then the LORD saw that the wickedness of man was great on the earth, and that every intent of the thoughts of his heart was only evil continually...But Noah found favor in the eyes of the LORD. Genesis 6:5, 8 NASB

Thus, man was preserved because of the righteousness of Noah and his family. Therefore, nearly two millennia after Adam, God reiterated his original and immutable plan to Noah.

And God blessed Noah and his sons and said to them, "Be fruitful and multiply, and fill the earth. And the fear of you and the terror of you shall be on every beast of the earth and on every bird of the sky; with everything that creeps on the ground, and all the fish of the sea, into your hand they are given." Genesis 9:1-2 NASB

Noah's sons

Noah had three sons named Shem, Ham, and Japheth.

In the course of time, Noah became a farmer and planted a vineyard. It was during this time that Noah's son Ham sinned against his father while Noah was drunk.

Little is said about the specific sin; however, it was deemed significant inasmuch as his brothers attempted to mitigate its effects. Nevertheless Ham would pay a tremendous price for his actions.

When Noah awoke from his wine, he said:

"Cursed be Canaan; a servant of servants he shall be to his brothers. Blessed be the LORD, the God of Shem; and let Canaan be his servant. May God enlarge Japheth, and let him dwell in the tents of Shem; and let Canaan be his servant." Genesis 9:25-27 NASB

Canaan was one of Ham's four sons.

Ham would be subservient to his brothers Shem and Japheth through his son Canaan.

Part of the curse upon Canaan would be the loss of his homeland to the offspring of Shem, beginning with Abraham.

However, the curse had other far-reaching ramifications.

Another of Ham's sons was named Cush.

Now Cush became the father of Nimrod; he became a mighty one on the earth. Genesis 10:8 NASB

Nimrod defied God's command

Not only would Nimrod become a great and renowned hunter, but his name also has the meanings of 'tyrant' and 'rebel.' Nimrod became a powerful leader of other rebellious followers.

And the beginning of his kingdom was Babel...in the land of Shinar. From that land he went forth into Assyria and built Nineveh... Genesis 10:10-11 NASB

The land of Shinar was located in Mesopotamia between the Tigris and Euphrates rivers. The Tigris and Euphrates rivers were listed as two 'riverheads' that watered the Garden of Eden. The land of Shinar was/is in the center of the Fertile Crescent and is currently known as Iraq.

Contrary to God's instructions for Noah's sons to 'replenish the earth...'

"Now the whole earth had one language and one speech. And it came to pass, as they (Nimrod and his followers) journeyed from the east, that they found a plain in the land of Shinar, and they dwelt there." Genesis 11:1-2 NKJV

Therefore, Nimrod's rebellion was to disobey God's command by settling in a particular place and maintaining unity of language.

Nimrod and his followers reveal their plan

And they said, "Come, let us build for ourselves a city, and a tower whose top will reach into heaven, and let us make for ourselves a name; lest we be scattered abroad over the face of the whole earth." Genesis 11:4 NASB

Their plan was exactly opposite to God's intent and instructions for mankind to replenish the earth.

Nimrod wanted to build both a city and a tower. According to the Hebrew language a tower represented pride, exaltation, boastfulness, and greatness. *'...whose top will reach into heaven'* reveals that Nimrod and his followers thought they were self-sufficient and didn't need God.

The phrase *'let us make for ourselves a name'* implied that the rebels were seeking fame and renown, while simultaneously flaunting their selfish purpose.

But God's immutable plan would prevail

So the LORD scattered them abroad from there over the face of the whole earth; and they stopped building the city. Genesis 11:8 NASB

The deserted city was named *'Babel'* which has several meaningful synonyms including 'mix,' 'mingle,' and 'confusion.'

However, renowned Hebrew lexicographers contend that the word *'Babel'* had its origin from the Hebrew *'balal'* which means 'gate of God.'

Both interpretations are entirely appropriate.

Subsequently, Nimrod and his followers migrated northward to build Nineveh.

The future of the land of Shinar

As we'll learn shortly, God wasn't done with the land of Shinar, or the deserted city of Babel.

As history progressed, three world kingdoms would come and go beginning with Egypt, then Assyria, and then Babylon which had just been overtaken by Media-Persia in 539 BC.

Shortly after Babylon's demise, the prophet Zechariah issued a proclamation relative to the future of the land of Shinar.

And so it was, an angel revealed to Zechariah that, in a far off day, Israel would be cleansed of evil, and the evil doers would be 'cut off' from the land.

Zechariah observed something departing (going forth) from the land. He inquired to the angel as to what it was that he was seeing.

"...and he said, 'it is a basket that is going forth.'"
Zechariah 5:6 NKJV

The departing basket was more specifically an ephah which is a bulk measuring container which holds approximately two-thirds bushel. On the top of the ephah was a lead cover to contain the contents of the ephah.

The lead cover represented a large round coin weighing approximately a talent, or 100 lbs.

Thus the ephah with its lead cover represented commerce, or mercantilism. Then the angel lifted the lead cover and revealed the contents of the ephah.

...and behold, a lead cover was lifted up; and this is a woman sitting inside the ephah. Then he said, "This is Wickedness!" And he threw her down into the middle of the ephah and cast the lead weight on its opening.
Zechariah 5:7-8 NASB

Then Zechariah saw two women lifting up the basket between earth and heaven, and he asked the angel where the women were taking the basket.

"And he said to me, 'To build a house for it in the land of Shinar; when it is ready, the basket will be set there on its base.'" Zechariah 5:11 NKJV

The 'house' represents a temple or palace which would be built in the future in the land of Shinar. The basket (ephah) would be set on its own base when the predetermined time arrives.

The prophecy reveals that the future commercial center of the world would be established where ancient Babel was, i.e. the land of Shinar.

Scripture leads one to conclude that the woman of wickedness in the ephah described by Zechariah is later described as the great harlot at the end of days.

"Mystery, Babylon the great, the mother of harlots and of the abominations of the earth." Revelation 17:5 NKJV

Harlotry, idolatry, and mercantilism

The prophet Zechariah had revealed that wickedness was placed in the measuring basket and headed for Shinar, in its time.

The Biblical definition of mercantilism is nearly identical with the contemporary meaning offered by Webster.

"...an economic system...to unify and increase the power and especially the monetary wealth of a nation by a strict governmental regulation of the entire national economy...a favorable balance of trade...and the establishment of foreign trading monopolies..."

Before exploring the meaning of the harlot and her fornication revealed in Scripture, let's build a wider foundation from other Old Testament writers.

The prophet Hosea had revealed that Ephraim (northern Israel) would shortly be overtaken by Assyria.

The major reason for her fall was due to harlotry, idolatry, and mercantilism. God provided a detailed example of such, and the required chastisement.

Israel played the harlot with her betrothed

The relationship between Hosea and Gomer (Hosea's wife) represented God's relationship with Israel. The unfaithfulness of Gomer would represent Israel's unfaithfulness to their betrothed, i.e. God.

"Go, take to yourself a wife of harlotry...for the land commits flagrant harlotry (spiritual adultery), forsaking the LORD." Hosea 1:2 NASB

The above verse reveals that such spiritual adultery was Israel's forsaking, or departing, from the LORD.

Then God explains to Hosea the relationship between harlotry and idolatry.

My people consult their wooden idol, and their diviner's wand informs them; for a spirit of harlotry has led them astray, and they have played the harlot, departing from their God. Hosea 4:12 NASB

Ephraim (Israel) rationalized her harlotry by believing her needs were being met by her lovers instead of God, her true provider.

"For she said, "I will go after my lovers, who give me my bread and my water, my wool and my flax, my oil and my drink...for she did not know that it was I who gave her the grain, the new wine, and the oil, and lavished on her silver and gold..." Hosea 2:5, 8 NASB

Replacing God's word with man's logic

All Israel had strayed from God's word.

The problems for both Ephraim (and Judah) were caused by relying on human logic instead of God's wisdom and commandments.

"Ephraim is oppressed and broken in judgment, because he willingly walked by human precept." Hosea 5:11 NKJV

Both Judah and Ephraim were deeply involved in mercantilism and the quest to increase their wealth. They didn't understand the consequences of such rationale.

And Ephraim said, "Surely I have become rich, I have found wealth for myself; in all my labors they will find in me no iniquity, which would be sin." Hosea 12:8 NASB

Not only had Israel become obsessed with increasing their wealth, they did not see that their quest for riches was sinful.

Confirmation of commercial Babylon

Both Ezekiel and Zechariah spoke of Babylon being the commercial center of the world. When Judah's king Jehoiachin was exiled to Babylon, the event was expressed metaphorically as an eagle carrying a twig.

"He plucked off the topmost of its young twigs and brought it to a land of merchants; he set it in a city of traders." Ezekiel 17:4 NASB

Thus Israel was imitating Babylon, the symbol of mercantilism, and by doing so was deeply involved in idolatry. Such activity was deemed to be, and labeled as, harlotry (spiritual adultery against God).

Israel would pay a heavy price for practicing the harlotry of mercantilism.

And we need always to keep in mind the following when studying God's dealing with Israel.

Now these things happened to them as an example, and they were written for our instruction, upon whom the ends of the ages have come. Therefore let him who thinks he stands take heed lest he fall. 1 Corinthians 10:11-12 NASB

Prophecy is pre-written history

Prophecy reveals God's plan for the future. As previously noted, prophecy typically has both short-term and long-term implications.

For example, several prophets including Hosea spoke in advance of Ephraim's imminent fall for their unfaithfulness.

And so it was, the chastisement for Ephraim's harlotry towards God was fulfilled by God's puppet Assyria, beginning in 722 BC.

In the same light, several prophets spoke in advance of Judah's imminent fall for their sin of unfaithfulness.

And so it was, Babylon's overrun of Judah began in 605 BC.

Israel's ultimate chastisement for their harlotry will occur just prior to Christ returning to end the great tribulation.

Recall, the future tribulation is called 'the time of Jacob's trouble.'

Harlotry was not confined to Israel

While Israel was the primary example of harlotry (spiritual adultery), all nations would be involved in harlotry, as defined in the Bible.

With that in mind, let's revisit the ultimate harlot in Revelation 17.

Near the end of the great tribulation, an angel spoke to John about this harlot.

"Come, I will show you the judgment of the great harlot who sits on many waters, with whom the kings of the earth committed fornication, and the inhabitants of the

earth were made drunk with the wine of her fornication."
Revelation 17:1-2 NKJV

The ultimate harlot is about to be judged. It is noted that she *'sits on many waters'* which indicates that she has ruling influence over the leaders of many nations.

The word 'harlot' in the above is from the Greek verb *porne* which means 'to sell,' particularly as merchants. *Porne* is synonymous with the Greek *piprasko* which means 'to travel beyond,' or 'to buy and sell merchandise in other lands.' Other synonyms include to 'trade' and 'engage in business.'

The word 'fornication' in the present context is from the Greek *porneia* which symbolically means idolatry. Since Christ is the bridegroom of the church, such fornication is against Christ in the form of spiritual adultery.

The future judgment of the great harlot

The Bible subsequently reveals that the ultimate harlot will be destroyed by the ten nation confederation of the seventh and final kingdom under the rule of the anti-Christ.

And then another profound prophecy is revealed relative to Babylon.

"And the woman whom you saw is the great city, which reigns over the kings of the earth." Revelation 17:18 NASB

This prophecy confirms and reinforces the prophecies of Zechariah, Jeremiah, and Ezekiel.

Recall, Zechariah spoke of the woman in the measuring basket headed for the land of Shinar where the basket would be set on its base, in God's timing. The woman was wickedness and represented commercialism (mercantilism).

The land of Shinar is a physical place and the base for the basket will be a physical structure.

Just as the city and tower in ancient Babel were physical, so will be the future city and tower, in the same location.

And just as Jeremiah spoke of the approaching desolation of ancient Babylon, the apostle John spoke of the approaching destruction of the future Babylon.

Babylon fell to the Medes and Persians in 539 BC after Jeremiah announced its fate. Again, Jeremiah's prophecy had both short-term and long-term implications.

After providing numerous details about Babylon's fate, Jeremiah was instructed to tell the Babylonians what was about to happen.

"So Jeremiah wrote in a book all the evil that would come upon Babylon..." Jeremiah 51:60 NKJV

God had instructed Jeremiah to send his servant to Babylon and read to them all the words in the 'book' about their fate.

...and say, "Thou, O LORD, hast promised concerning this place to cut it off, so that there will be nothing dwelling in it, whether man or beast, but it will be a perpetual desolation." Jeremiah 51:62 NASB

Then Jeremiah instructed his servant how to dispose of the book.

"And it will come about as soon as you finish reading this scroll (book), you will tie a stone to it and throw it into the middle of the Euphrates (river), and say, 'Just so shall Babylon sink down and not rise again, because of the calamity that I am going to bring upon her...'" Jeremiah 51:63-64 NASB

Get out of there!

Just before Jeremiah's scroll detailing Babylon's destruction was cast into the River Euphrates, God's people were told to flee.

Flee from the midst of Babylon, and each of you save his life! Do not be destroyed in her punishment, for this is the LORD's time of vengeance; He is going to render recompense to her...We applied healing to Babylon, but she was not healed; forsake her...for her judgment has reached to heaven. Jeremiah 51:6, 9 NASB

Jeremiah shortly thereafter stresses the importance of distancing oneself from Babylon and everything she stands for.

"Come forth from her midst, My people, and each of you save yourselves from the fierce anger of the LORD." Jeremiah 51:45 NASB

Babylon's final destruction would include both her idolatrous system and her physical city and tower.

And one last warning will be given just before the future Babylon is destroyed.

And I heard another voice from heaven, saying, "Come out of her, my people, that you may not participate in her sins and that you may not receive of her plagues; for her sins have piled up as high as heaven, and God has remembered her iniquities." Revelation 18:4-5 NASB

The message is unquestionably clear. Harlotry, idolatry, and fornication (spiritual adultery) expressed in commerce and materialism is scheduled to be utterly destroyed forever. The warning is to escape the insatiable appetite for 'merchandise' of all kinds. It is simply a matter of priorities.

The physical destruction of future Babylon, as described in Revelation, is eerily similar to the words used by Jeremiah when the 'book' was cast into the river Euphrates never to rise again.

And a strong angel took up a stone like a great millstone and threw it into the sea, saying, "Thus will Babylon, the great city, be thrown down with violence, and will not be found any longer." Revelation 18:21 NASB

Many people can identify with the idolatrous Babylon; however, few give much thought to the future physical city of Babylon.

Examples of Babylon today

The World Trade Center collapsed in 'an hour' on 9-11-2001. Our leader's resolve at that time was to quickly bring the stock market back in operation to prove to the world that America was financially strong and resilient.

The World Trade Center has since been replaced with 1 World Trade Center, or perhaps better known as the Freedom Tower. Its height is 1,776 feet.

It must not be forgotten that on 9-11-1683 the Ottoman Empire was derailed in Vienna. That stopped the western leg of the Roman Empire. Bin Laden used that date to rekindle the war.

But even a taller building than America's Freedom Tower is found in Dubai. It is called Burj Khalifa which has 160 stories with a height of 2,723 feet.

A lesser known building in progress is the Kingdom Tower in Jeddah Arabia. The Kingdom Tower has presently completed 23 stories and is scheduled for completion in 2019 or 2020. Its height is planned to be 3,250 feet.

In a CNN article dated 11 January 2018 the Chief Executive Officer of Jeddah Economic Company made a statement that sounded more like Western Civilization than Eastern ways.

"With this deal, we will reach new, as yet unheard of highs in real estate development, and will fulfill the company's objective of creating a world-class urban center that offers an advanced lifestyle, so that Jeddah may have a new iconic landmark…"

And lastly there are plans for a city/tower reaching a height of 3,780 feet. It is interestingly named 'The Bride.' It will be by far the tallest building in the world.

It will be a complex of four conjoined towers resulting in what is called the world's first 'vertical city.'

Where will 'The Bride' be built?

'The Bride' is to rise in Iraq's oil-rich Basra Province.

Recall, Iraq is situated between the Tigris and Euphrates rivers in the land of Shinar.

Various news agencies have recently reported on the world's tallest buildings.

The rebuilding of 'Babylon' called 'The Bride' in the same place where it all started with Nimrod should capture the interest of all.

It would be beneficial to read the leaves on the fig tree i.e. examine current events and weigh them against Biblical teachings.

Will the summation of such examination confirm Jeremiah's message, 'Get out of There!?'

Here comes the bride

The Basra province in Iraq is locally known as 'the bride of the gulf' owing to its fertility in growing vegetation and agriculture products. Basra is also recognized as Iraq's main port.

The proposed city/tower will include a large 'veil' designed to shade parks, gardens, and other smaller buildings at lower levels.

There are numerous visual projections of the planned city/tower readily available.

Significant people of the East

Both Arabia and Iraq are considered to be located in the 'East.' The Hebrew definition of the 'East' has both geographical and cultural (temporal) meanings. Cultural applications of the 'East' include the culture of nomadic tribes of Syria and Northern Africa. The Biblical terms for such cultures include 'Sons of the East' or 'them of the East.'

The most significant people of the East include the sons of Ishmael, and the sons of Abraham and Keturah.

Recall how the Angel of the LORD described Ishmael to his mother while he was still in the womb.

"He shall be a wild man; his hand shall be against every man, and everyman's hand against him. And he shall dwell in the presence of all his brethren." Genesis 16:12 NASB

'Wild donkey' is from the Hebrew 'onager.'

God gave Job more insight on the characteristics of the onager; the wild man that Ishmael would be.

"Who set the wild donkey free? Who loosed the bonds of the onager, whose home I have made the wilderness, and the barren land his dwelling? He scorns the tumult of the city; he does not heed the shouts of the driver." Job 39:5-7 NKJV

The sons of Ishmael were the beginnings of the tribes of Arabia.

The sons of Abraham and Keturah were likewise sent to the East.

Now Abraham gave all that he had to Isaac; but to the sons of his concubines, Abraham gave gifts while he was still living, and sent them away from his son Isaac eastward, to the land of the east. Genesis 25:5-6 NASB

'Eastern ways' were in conflict with God's standard of righteousness and justice revealed to His chosen nation of Israel.

In fact, when Isaiah relayed to the Israelites why God was displeased with them, he explained God's position.

For Thou has abandoned Thy people, the house of Jacob, because they are filled with influences from the east, and they are soothsayers like the Philistines, and they strike bargains with the children of foreigners.
Isaiah 2:6 NASB

Foreigners can also mean 'gentile,' 'outsider,' and/or 'alien.'

'Soothsayers' means 'to act covertly;' 'to practice magic and divination,' and lastly, the Israelites were 'placing priorities on riches.'

Thus, according to the Bible, God did not want His people to adopt and practice 'eastern ways.'

The animosity between Ishmael, identified with Arabia, and Isaac, the progenitor of Israel through his son Jacob, began in Isaac's early days.

Recall the significant event that occurred at Isaac's weaning celebration when Ishmael was in his early teen years.

And the child grew and was weaned, and Abraham made a great feast on the day that Isaac was weaned. Now Sarah saw the son of Hagar the Egyptian, whom she had borne to Abraham, mocking (scoffing). Genesis 21:8-9 NASB

Ishmael's actions were so significant that nearly two millennia later Paul recounted that event and stressed that such a relationship prevailed in his day.

The father of 'the bride'

It is a significant Biblical truth that there is animosity between the offspring of Ishmael and the offspring of Isaac. Moreover, according to the Bible, there was/is/ and will be animosity between and among the sons of Ishmael.

Isaac's father Abraham is also the father of the current age church which is the Bride of God's Son Jesus.

Therefore, be sure that it is those who are of faith that are sons of Abraham...And if you belong to Christ, then you are Abraham's offspring, heirs according to promise. Galatians 3:7, 29 NASB

Paul provided even more details in his letter to the Christians in Rome.

...For they are not all Israel who are descended from Israel; neither are they all children because they are Abraham's descendants, but: "THROUGH ISAAC YOUR DESCENDANTS WILL BE NAMED." That is, it is not the

children of the flesh (Ishmael) who are children of God, but the children of the promise (Isaac) are regarded as descendants. Romans 9:6b-5 NASB

The Bible explicitly states numerous times that the immutable and everlasting covenant that God made with Abraham is perpetuated through His son Isaac, not Ishmael.

Ishmael was Abraham's physical son born through Hagar, the bond woman. Seeing Ishmael was born before Isaac, Abraham suggested that Ishmael receive the promise and perpetuate the covenant.

But God said, "No, but Sarah your wife shall bear you a son, and you shall call his name Isaac; and I will establish My covenant with him (whom Sarah will bear to you at this season next year) for an everlasting covenant for his descendants after him..." Genesis 16:19, 21 NASB

And recall, Ishmael and his offspring became the tribes of Arabia and 'those of the East.'

The animosity between Ishmael's offspring and those not sharing the 'ways of the East' was exhibited on 9-11 when it was learned that 15 of the 19 who flew the aircraft on that day were from Saudi Arabia. Their primary target was the World Trade Center towers.

There has also been strife among 'those of the East' exhibited in several ways. For example, in battles during

Israel's past history, God would set those of the East against each other.

Recall, the battle between Israel's judge Gideon and Midian, a son of Abraham and Keturah. Gideon employed just 300 troops against many thousand Midianites.

And when they blew 300 trumpets, the LORD set the sword of one against another even throughout the whole army, and the army fled... Judges 7:22 NASB

Prophecies about to become reality

The prophet Ezekiel reveals the identity of seven of the final ten nation confederation that in the latter days will be drawn by God to Israel for a great battle.

Those nations include Meshech, Tubal, Persia (Iran), Cush (a son of Ham), Libya, Gomer, and Togarmah. These nations are either physically, culturally, or both, from the 'East.' In fact, Meshech, Tubal, Gomer, and Togarmah are all located in present day Turkey.

It has been previously stated that wickedness, represented by a woman, manifested in mercantilism, will be transported to its future base in the land of Shinar in God's timing.

It has also been stated previously that the woman in the final days of this age was *'sitting on a scarlet beast which was full of names of blasphemy, having seven heads and*

239

ten horns.' The woman represented both the culture of mercantilism as well as a future physical city.

Interestingly, the Bible states that the final ten nation federation will destroy the woman and the city she represents.

"And the ten horns which you saw, and the beast, these will hate the harlot and will make her desolate and naked, and will eat her flesh and will burn her up with fire. For God has put it in their hearts to execute His purpose by having a common purpose ...until the words of God should be fulfilled." Revelation 17:16-17 NASB

Now, the ten horns are the same as the ten toes in Nebuchadnezzar's dream.

When Daniel interpreted the dream, he revealed that the feet and toes were composed of iron mixed with clay, meaning that the member nations of the final world kingdom would be divided; being partly strong and partly brittle.

Therefore, current events combined with Biblical history and prophecy raise several interesting questions.

For illustrative purposes, consider three representative nations, i.e. Turkey, Saudi Arabia, and Persia (Iran).

Is there unity or division between these nations? In other words, is there continuity of culture, politics, and religion between these three nations?

For example, politically, Saudi Arabia is considered to be an absolute monarchy, while Iran is a theocracy. Turkey, on the other hand, is considered to be a pseudo representative democratic republic.

And then, might there be in the future cultural or religious strife internally within each of these nations?

While these three representative nations are predominantly Islamic, there exist different sects within them, primarily Shia and Sunni.

However, recall the previous Scripture quoted:

"For God has put it in their hearts to execute His purpose by having a common purpose...until the words of God should be fulfilled." Revelation 17:17 NASB

For sure, the whole world is anxious to learn who the father of 'The Bride' is.

Again, it's time to study and reflect on the leaves of the fig tree.

Chapter 11

The Relevance of the 'Time' Dimension

'Time' is a dimension that God provided to enable man to understand His plan for those created in His image. Time had a beginning and, after running its course, will cease to be.

Time is a linear function from beginning to end with two aspects, i.e. a point on the linear span called 'when' and a period of time called 'how long' defined as a period occurring between two points on the span.

God displayed His unfathomable sovereign power in creation prior to the advent of time, which He provided just prior to the creation of Adam.

Paul confirmed that God's plan for His chosen was devised before time began. God would reveal His plan and its components in exact order and in exact timing for man to be able to comprehend what He was doing.

God, who has saved us and called us to a holy life – not because of anything we have done but because of his own purpose and grace. This grace was given us in Christ Jesus before the beginning of time.
2 Timothy 1:9 NIV

Thus God's plan for man was determined long before the dimension of time was established.

The study of the time dimension can be challenging, inasmuch as there are 27 Hebrew words translated 'time' and 25 Greek words translated 'time.'

The beginning of time

The Book of Genesis provides details on the origin of time. Time was provided on the 4th 'day' of creation.

And God said, "Let there be lights in the expanse of the sky to separate the day from the night, and let them serve as signs to mark seasons and days and years..."
Genesis 1:14 NIV

The Hebrew for 'seasons' means 'appointment' which, among other things, would signal the timing of the future Jewish feast days to be revealed in God's time. The dimension of time would also help explain many prophecies which were expressed in terms of the time dimension.

The Hebrew for 'day' does in fact mean 'time,' either between two points on the linear time span or a specific point of time on that span as previously defined. 'Years' means a 'revolution of time,' or 'to return,' and/or 'repeat.' Such describes the earth's annual journey around the sun.

Notice that there would be lights, i.e. plural, meaning luminous bodies. Light in the singular had been provided earlier.

Now the earth was formless and empty, darkness was over the surface of the deep, and the Spirit of God was hovering over the waters. And God said, "Let there be light," and there was light. Genesis 1:2-3 NIV

'Light' in this case means 'illumination' or 'enlightenment.' Such light defines the presence of God and His glory.

God is not constrained by the time dimension

"For a thousand years in Your sight are like yesterday when it is past, and like a watch in the night." Psalm 90:4 NKJV

The Hebrew for 'thousand' is the quantity of years as we know it today; however, a related synonym is 'innumerable.'

'Yesterday' does indicate a day as we know it and a 'watch in the night' is from the Hebrew defining a four hour time period.

The Apostle Peter reiterated that God's days and years were not limited to the same finite dimensions as He provided to man.

But do not forget this one thing...With the Lord a day is like a thousand years, and a thousand years are like a day. 2 Peter 3:8 NIV

The Greek word for thousand also has several meanings similar to the Hebrew including a literal finite thousand or 'innumerable.'

The same Greek word for thousand *(chilioi)* is found in the following:

And I saw the souls of those who had been beheaded because of their testimony for Jesus and because of the word of God...They came to life and reigned with Christ a thousand years. (The rest of the dead did not come to life until the thousand years were ended). Revelation 20:4b-5 NIV

The meaning for 'thousand years' in the above is widely disputed. While many believe it means 'innumerable,' pre-millennialism regards the thousand year period as strictly literal.

Other Scripture references tend to validate the literal interpretation of 'thousand' in the foregoing passage.

They will trample on the holy city for 42 months. And I will give power to my two witnesses, and they will prophesy for 1,260 days... Revelation 11:2b-3 NIV

The three and one half years, i.e. the second half of the seven year tribulation period is exactly forty two prophetic months of thirty days each, and one thousand two hundred and sixty days is exactly forty two months or three and half prophetic years.

The relevance of time becomes very intriguing when considering that the present church age defines the time gap between Daniel's 69th and 70th prophetic weeks. A 'week' in the Hebrew is seven, therefore, seventy weeks equates to 490 years. The 70th week of seven years defines the rapidly approaching tribulation.

Time is finite

Recall, the time dimension can be expressed as either a point on the linear time span, or a period on the span determined by a beginning or ending point.

If 'when' is the object, the Greek base is predominately *kairos* which means an 'appointed, set, fixed, or definite' point on the linear time span. It can be further defined as a time of accomplishment of foreordained events.

However, if 'how long' is the object of time in question, the Greek word predominately used is *chronos,* meaning an 'interval,' or 'period' of measured time.

Let's begin by examining several examples of *kairos* defining the word 'time' in the New Testament.

When John was sent to prison shortly after baptizing Jesus, He announced:

"The time has come (fulfilled)," he said. "The kingdom of God is near... Mark 1:15 NIV

'Time' in this verse means the 'pre-appointed, set point, or event' on the time span of history had arrived. 'Fulfilled' means 'completed.' In other words, the time period leading up to the arrival of the Messiah was completed.

Paul likewise spoke of a point on the time span as he described the redemption made possible by Christ.

And he made known to us the mystery of his will according to his good pleasure, which he purposed in Christ, to be put into effect when the times (kairos) will have reached their fulfillment – to bring all things in heaven and on earth together under one head, even Christ. Ephesians 1:9-10 NIV

Paul explained that the predetermined (set) time for the advent of the Messiah had arrived. Likewise, the mystery of redemption was revealed at the exact preordained time in history. And again, 'fulfillment' means 'complete.'

In his letter to Titus, similar to his letter to Timothy, Paul also acknowledged that God's promise for eternal life was devised before time began, but he also revealed the mystery of redemption at the exact (proper) time as history unfolded.

...which God, who does not lie, promised before the beginning of time (chronos), and at his appointed season (Kairos) he brought his word to light... Titus 1:2-3 NIV

Notice that two definitions of 'time' are included in the same sentence.

'Appointed season' also carries the connotation of the present time, or time of opportunity.

When Paul addressed the crowd at Athens, he also spoke of God's sovereignty relative to the time dimension.

"And He (God) has made from one blood every nation of men to dwell on all the face of the earth, and has determined their pre-appointed times (kairos) and the boundaries of their dwellings..." Acts 17:26 NKJV

'Determined' and 'pre-appointed' are also synonyms for 'ordained.'

Then there is an excellent example of *(chronos)* in Galatians.

In this example Paul used the analogy of a new Christian being similar to a child. A child, even though being a legal heir, was likened to a slave until a certain level of maturity was reached.

"...but (a child) is under guardians and stewards until the time (kairos) appointed by the father. Even so we, when we were children, were in bondage under the elements of the world. But when the fullness of the time (chronos) had come, God sent forth His Son..." Galatians 4:1-4 NKJV

The phrase 'the time appointed' has been discussed, and the context of the phrase 'fullness of the time' means a specific period of time measured by the succession of events, the time of preordained accomplishments. And recall, 'fullness' means 'completion' or 'end.'

Two words used for 'time' are included in the following, i.e. *(chilioi)* meaning a thousand years and also *(chronos)* is used to define a short time period.

He seized the dragon, that ancient serpent, who is the devil, or Satan, and bound him for a thousand (chilioi) years.. After that he must be set free for a short time (chronos). Revelation 20:2-3 NIV

Solomon attempted to place events and time in perspective

A millennium prior to Paul's speech at Athens, Solomon spoke of God's sovereignty relative to time – present and future.

There is a time for everything, and a season for every activity under heaven. Ecclesiastes 3:1 NIV

'Season' in this verse likewise means in Hebrew an 'appointed' or 'determined' time. The word 'time' in the present context means the 'right,' or 'proper' time.

And then Solomon spoke of the same judgment as did Paul.

"God will bring to judgment both the righteous and the wicked, for there will be a (right) time for every activity, a time for every deed." Ecclesiastes 3:17 NIV

Increments of time shorter than a year are used in Scripture

The Bible also uses increments of time less than a year including month, day and hour.

...but now he (God) commands all people everywhere to repent. For he has set a day when he will judge the world with justice... Acts 17:30b-31 NIV

The 'day' of the future judgment of the world was ordained before the dimension of time existed. The word 'day' in this context definitely means a set day.

Then I saw another angel flying in midair, and he had the eternal gospel to proclaim to those who live on the earth..."Fear God and give him glory, because the hour of his judgment has come..." Revelation 14:6-7 NIV

'Hour' is the Greek *hora* meaning a division of time recurring at fixed intervals.

The same *'hora'* is used in the following:

"Release the four angels who are bound at the great river Euphrates." And the four angels who had been kept ready for this very hour and day and month and year were released to kill a third of mankind."
Revelation 9:14b-15 NIV

Time of the end

The phrase 'time of the end' typically refers to the return of Christ after the seven year tribulation period.

Josephus outlined in great detail the atrocities of Antiochus Epiphanes of the Seleucid Empire, who is referred to as king of the north in the book of Daniel. Antiochus was the precursor of the future king of the final world kingdom, i.e. the anti-Christ.

Recall that some of the Jews would not bow down to Antiochus at the cost of their lives.

Some of the wise will stumble, so that they may be refined, purified and made spotless until the time of the end, for it will still come at the appointed time. Daniel 11:35 NIV

This verse reveals such suffering and oppression of the Jews in the 2nd century BC will be experienced up to the 'time of the end' because it is still for the 'appointed time.'

'Time' in the above refers to the 'right' or 'proper' point in time on the linear time span.

We'll see shortly that the 'time of the end' can refer also to the end of the world system as we know it. The term 'appointed time' means a 'pre-determined time.'

The 'time of the end' is also a significant teaching in the New Testament. Jesus' disciples were very interested in the time Jesus would return to establish His kingdom.

As Jesus was sitting on the Mount of Olives, the disciples came to him privately. "Tell us," they said, "when will this happen, and what will be the sign of your coming and of the end of the age?" Matthew 24:3 NIV

'End' does in fact mean 'termination.' Interestingly 'end' in this context is from the Greek *(aion)* which is the same word used for 'age.' Therefore, each age has an ending, except the new heaven and new earth.

Jesus addressed the disciple's question relative to the end of the current age.

"You will hear of wars and rumors of wars, but see to it that you are not alarmed. Such things must happen, but the end is still to come." Matthew 24:6 NIV

Wars are to be expected during the present age, but they do not define the 'end.' In fact Jesus said that such things were just the beginning of sorrows. The use of 'sorrows' describe the pain experienced in childbirth. When such pain begins it will accelerate until the birth occurs.

Then Jesus provided a glimpse of when the end would take place.

"And this gospel of the kingdom will be preached in the whole world as a testimony to all nations, and then the end will come." Matthew 24:14 NIV

The Bible reveals many 'signs of the times' provided for man to recognize the reality of prophetic Scripture but skeptics were not convinced. Recall Jesus' words to the Pharisees and Sadducees when they asked for a sign of Jesus' authority.

He replied, "When evening comes, you say, 'It will be fair weather, for the sky is red,' and in the morning, 'Today it will be stormy, for the sky is red and overcast.' You know how to interpret the appearance of the sky, but you cannot interpret the signs of the times." Matthew 16:2-3 NIV

And while many 'signs of the times,' or the set time for Messiah's return, were listed by Jesus as He described future events such as in the Olivet Discourse, many signs were provided hundreds of years prior.

Consider the following prophetic message given to Daniel, relative to the mid-point of the future tribulation.

He (anti-Christ) will speak against the Most High and oppress his saints and try to change the set times and the laws. The saints will be handed over to him for a time, times and half a time. Daniel 7:25 NIV

The Hebrew for 'change' means to 'alter' or be 'diverse,' while 'set times' imply appointed times such as Jewish or Christian holidays. The word 'time' in the phrase 'time and times and half a time' means a literal year.

Thus the anti-Christ during the tribulation will attempt to alter or eliminate the feast days of the Jews. Even in this current age there are attempts to marginalize days honoring Christ.

The word 'Christmas' for example, is becoming politically incorrect because the thought or mention of Christ may offend some.

The Bible tells succinctly what the Christian should be doing during the time period preceding the return of Christ.

"See then that you walk circumspectly, not as fools but as wise, redeeming the time (kairos), because the days are evil." Ephesians 5:16 NKJV

The Greek basis for 'time' in this verse is very revealing. It not only means 'season,' but it has the rich meaning of a 'period of opportunity.' The Greek for 'redeeming' means not to allow the moment to pass by unheeded, but to make the best use of the time knowing Christ will return at a specific, pre-appointed, preordained time to judge the earth.

When will be the end?

It is an absolute Biblical certainty that the world as we know it will come to an end. The age of the Church is nearing completion. This age will be followed by seven years of great tribulation, ending with the return of Christ to establish His earthly kingdom in Jerusalem.

"No one knows about that day or hour, not even the angels in heaven, nor the Son, but only the Father." Matthew 24:36 NIV

'Hour' in this verse does in fact mean a division of the day; it is as we know it.

Jesus very clearly states that the day and hour of His return had been determined before time began, but not revealed.

Jesus continued by stating that mankind in general gives little thought or priority to the end of this age. Life goes on as if the problems of the world will work themselves out without divine intervention.

"As it was in the days of Noah, so it will be at the coming of the Son of Man. For in the days before the flood, people were eating and drinking, marrying and giving in marriage, up to

the day Noah entered the ark; and they knew nothing about what would happen until the flood came and took them all away. That is how it will be at the coming of the Son of Man." Matthew 24:37-39 NIV

The world will be taken by surprise at Christ's return.

"Therefore keep watch, because you do not know the day or the hour (in which the Son of Man is coming)." Matthew 25:13 NIV

After Jesus' resurrection, and just prior to His ascension, the disciples asked if it was the time for Him to restore Israel as a nation.

So when they met together, they asked him, "Lord, are you at this time going to restore the kingdom to Israel?" He said to them: "It is not for you to know the times or dates the Father has set by his own authority." Acts 1:6-7 NIV

Recall, 'times or dates' mean the 'exact,' 'set,' 'predetermined' time that Christ will return to earth.

Time will be no more

This chapter began with the creation of the solar system which provided man with a means to place 'time' in its proper perspective. The day will come when the sun will no longer be needed and time will be no more.

After the church age, after the tribulation, after the millennial kingdom, and after the earth is renewed, there will be no need for the time dimension.

The solar system created for man's benefit in Genesis 1:14 will no longer be needed.

There will be no more night. They will not need the light of a lamp or the light of the sun, for the Lord God will give them light. Revelation 22:5 NIV

And for those who think this life is the most significant time of man's odyssey:

"Man born of woman is of few days and full of trouble. He springs up like a flower and withers away; like a fleeting shadow, he does not endure." Job 14:1-2 NIV

The time of this present life is but a fleeting moment compared with eternity, when time will be no more.

Chapter 12

The Day of the LORD

The phrase the 'day of the Lord' is found numerous times in both Old and New Testaments.

The Hebrew for 'day' is the same word for 'time' which, as previously explained, can be either a point on the linear time span or a period of time on that span depending on the context.

The general implication for the phrase the 'day of the Lord' involves God's wrath and judgment. It is a dark time in history when the disobedience of man has run its course and God's attribute of justice will be unleashed.

Other words describing the day of the Lord include 'vengeance,' 'anger,' 'wrath,' 'destruction,' 'calamity,' and 'slaughter.'

The day of the Lord frequently also has duel applications, i.e. it may have a short-term application which serves as an example of the future judgment called the tribulation which will occur at the end of the church age. If the application is near-term, the events serve as wake up calls for the future.

A good example was the destruction of the World Trade Center. The death toll in that event approximated 3,000. During the future great day of the Lord, the death toll will be 1,000,000 for each life lost on 9-11.

The day of the Lord can apply to specific people groups, individual nations, or cities such as Israel's capital city Jerusalem. However, the day of the Lord, even if applicable to a short-term situation, typically points to the final great day of the Lord which is imminent and applies to all nations.

Divine vengeance is required of a Just God

God's vengeance will be poured out on all who disobey His commands; whether it is His chosen nation Israel or the nations that mistreat Israel.

Just prior to Israel taking possession of Canaan, God spoke to Moses and foretold of Israel's future disobedience. He told Moses to write in a song beforehand how they would act, as a witness to them. Then Moses was to read it to them so they would understand that their chastisement was just, inasmuch as they had been forewarned.

"And when many disasters and difficulties come upon them, this song will testify against them because it will not be forgotten by their descendants. I know what they are

disposed to do, even before I bring them into the land I promised them..." Deuteronomy 31:21 NIV

And then God told Moses in explicit detail how Israel would behave throughout their history, along with the consequences of their unfaithfulness.

When they disobeyed, they would bring on themselves God's vengeance.

"It is mine to avenge; I will repay. In due time their foot will slip...The LORD will judge his people...I will take vengeance on my adversaries and repay those who hate me." Deuteronomy 32:35a, 36a, 41b NIV

The world is in denial

God's wrath will fall not only on Israel, but on all nations that abused His chosen people or marginalized His word.

For example, the United Nations does not recognize Jerusalem as Israel's capital because it is such a controversial issue. God, however, has chosen Jerusalem as Israel's capital forever.

Providentially the United States has recently taken steps to recognize Jerusalem as Israel's rightful capital, and such efforts have been met with world wide opposition.

In addition, there is much controversy centered on ownership of the Temple Mount between the seeds of Isaac and Ishmael.

Such issues can only be resolved in the day of the Lord. Man is totally incompetent to handle such issues as long as the battle of the brothers, Ishmael and Isaac, rages on.

The naivety of the world's leaders is beyond comprehension. Even during the recent presidential campaign, the candidates proclaimed that America's greatest days lie ahead and they had the wisdom and power to make that a reality. Even professing Christians campaigned on such foolishness.

The day of the Lord will unleash God's wrath

Job spoke of the wicked of all nations being reserved for the future day of doom and wrath.

"For the wicked are reserved for the day of doom; they shall be brought out on the day of wrath." Job 21:30 NKJV

Isaiah spoke much of the future day of God's wrath on the wicked.

See, the day of the LORD is coming – a cruel day, with wrath and fierce anger... Isaiah 13:9 NIV

The issue of God's wrath has been experienced by the disobedient throughout history, and His wrath is awaiting all the wicked on that great and mighty day of the LORD at Christ's return.

Those who are treasuring up God's wrath for themselves are unrepentant. Their future judgment will be righteous and will be executed according to one's own deeds.

The day of the Lord according to Isaiah

We will report the words of the prophets that spoke of the day of the Lord in the order that they are listed in the Bible.

Isaiah addressed Israel's sin and inevitable judgment, prior to condemning the nations.

The LORD Almighty has a day in store for all the proud and lofty...They are full of superstitions from the East... The arrogance of man will be brought low and the pride of men humbled; the LORD alone will be exalted in that day... Isaiah 2:6a, 12, 17 NIV

'Superstitions from the East' includes the worship of pagan gods and idols, such as Abraham was instructed to forsake when he was told to go to a new land that God would show him.

Israel was also reminded of their sin of pride, and was told that such pride would be brought down in humility. Only their God was worthy of exaltation.

The following words of God reflect His growing anger toward future Babylon, and subsequently to all nations for their pride and lawlessness.

Wail, for the day of the LORD is near; it will come like destruction from the Almighty...I will punish the world for its evil...I will put an end to the arrogance of the haughty... Therefore I will make the heavens tremble; and the earth will shake from its place at the wrath of the LORD Almighty, in the day of his burning anger. Isaiah 13:6, 11, 13 NIV

'I will punish the world...I will put an end to the arrogance...I will make the heavens tremble...'

Unrepentant pride and arrogance is oft times made obvious when a nation's leader uses the words 'I will.'

But there is more, especially relative to the nations' respect and treatment of the 'Apple of God's eye,' i.e. Israel.

Come near, you nations, and listen; pay attention, you peoples! Let the earth hear, and all that is in it...The LORD is angry with all nations...For the LORD has a day of vengeance (revenge, retaliation), a year of retribution, to uphold Zion's cause (controversy). Isaiah 34:1-2, 8 NIV

The day of the Lord is a sure thing and is approaching quickly. Such prophecy as presented is absolute history written in advance and will certainly affect America.

Do you think perhaps the president will devise a strategy to confront this monumental issue?

The day of the Lord according to Jeremiah

When Judah's seventy year captivity had ended in 539 BC, God warned His people to flee from Babylon so that He could punish that nation for their sin.

This is what the LORD says: "See, I will stir up the spirit of a destroyer against Babylon...Flee from Babylon! It is time for the LORD's vengeance; he will pay her what she deserves. Babylon was a gold cup in the LORD's hand; she made the whole earth drunk...therefore they have now gone mad...her judgment reaches to the skies..." Jeremiah 51:1a, 6a, 7-9 NIV

Vengeance in this context is closely related to the previous definitions, but vindictiveness also plays a part, while 'pay her' in the present context adds the meaning of 'recompense.'

Again, the above Scripture has both short-term and long-term application. The short-term relates to the Medes defeating Babylon and freeing Judah from captivity; while the long-term relates to future Babylon, the great whore to be destroyed at the end of the tribulation.

Note the parallel Scripture passages from the final book in the Bible.

Then I heard another voice from heaven say: "Come out of her, my people...for her sins are piled up to heaven and God has remembered her crimes...give back to her as she has given..." Revelation 18:4-6 NIV

'Give back to her' means to 'recompense,' 'repay,' 'render' something necessary to fulfill an obligation.

Jeremiah reminded all that the future great tribulation was named after, and directed primarily to, His chosen nation.

"Alas! For that day is great, so that none is like it; and it is the time of Jacob's trouble..." Jeremiah 30:7 NKJV

The day of the Lord according to Ezekiel

The following verses relate to both Jerusalem's near-term destruction by Nebuchadnezzar, as well as long-term implications during the 'time of Jacob's trouble' just prior to Christ's return.

"Now upon you I will soon pour out My fury, and spend My anger upon you...I will repay you according to your ways...Their silver and their gold will not be able to deliver them in the day of the wrath of the LORD...and according to what they deserve I will judge them..."
Ezekiel 7:8-9, 19, 27 NKJV

Notice the 'I will' proclamations; 'I will soon pour out...' 'I will repay you...' 'I will judge them....' God's wrath was/

will be totally justified, i.e. 'repay,' and 'according to what they deserve.'

God proclaims that Israel, or any nation that depends on their financial prowess to deliver them, will be powerless in His day of wrath.

After countless warnings God justified His actions.

"I looked for a man among them who would build up the wall and stand before me in the gap on behalf of the land... but I found none. So I will pour out my wrath on them and consume them with my fiery anger, bringing down on their own heads (recompensed) all they have done..."
Ezekiel 22:30-31 NIV

No one would intercede for Jerusalem's sin. 'Wrath' is synonymous with 'indignation.'

God was/and is very longsuffering with His people. He reminded them of His wrath taken out on their enemy, i.e. Egypt, even though He had turned His wrath away from Israel many times for their deserved iniquities.

...their hearts were not loyal to him, they were not faithful to his covenant. Yet he was merciful...Time after time he restrained his anger and did not stir up his full wrath. Psalm 37-38 NIV

However, Israel did not remember God's power and wrath on Egypt when He redeemed them from bondage.

They did not remember his power – the day he redeemed them from the oppressor, the day he displayed his miraculous signs in Egypt...He unleashed against them his hot anger, his wrath, indignation and hostility...
Psalm 78:42-43, 49 NIV

The short-term message was directed to Judah and Jerusalem, with future implication to all nations.

The day of the Lord according to Joel

Joel offered much more detail on the day of the Lord.

Alas for that day! For the day of the LORD is near; it will come like destruction (violence, havoc, ruin) from the Almighty...The day of the LORD is great; it is dreadful (to be feared). Who can endure it? Joel 1:15, 2:11 NIV

Joel was subsequently told to warn Israel of the coming Day of Judgment. The following also has both short-term and long-term application.

Blow the trumpet in Zion; sound the alarm on my holy hill. Let all who live in the land tremble, for the day of the LORD is coming. It is close at hand – a day of darkness and gloom...such as never was of old nor ever will be in ages to come. Joel 2:1-2 NIV

And then Joel describes the future great day of the Lord when all nations will be gathered to be judged in the Valley of Jehoshaphat.

"I will also gather all nations, and bring them down to the valley of Jehoshaphat; and I will enter into judgment with them there on account of My people, My heritage Israel, whom they have scattered among the nations; they have also divided up My land...for there I will sit to judge all the surrounding nations...for the day of the LORD is near (at hand) in the valley of decision." Joel 3:2, 12, 14 NKJV

Note the 'I will' actions that God will take, i.e. 'I will gather...' 'I will enter into judgment...' 'I will sit to judge all nations...' The judgment in the present context is retribution for how the nations treated Israel.

Of particular interest is that one of the major sins of the nations was to divide the land that God had gifted to Israel. Even today the proposed division of Israel is the only suggested remedy for the problems in the Middle East offered by recent presidents of America. What a price to pay for such naivety.

The day of the Lord according to Amos

Israel had it all backwards.

This is what the LORD says to the house of Israel... "Woe to you who long for the day of the LORD! That day will be darkness, not light. It will be as though a man fled from a lion only to meet a bear, as though he entered his house and rested his hand on the wall only to have a snake

bite him. Will not the day of the LORD be darkness, not light...?" Amos 5:4, 18-20 NIV

The Israelites mistakenly thought that, inasmuch as they were God's chosen nation, their disobedience would be overlooked. They instead reasoned that they would be victorious in the sight of the nations. They were, in fact, looking forward in anxious anticipation to the day of the Lord.

The day of the Lord according to Obadiah

Obadiah prophesied to Edom in the 9th century BC.

"For the day of the LORD upon all the nations is near (shortly, nigh, at hand); as you have done, it shall be done to you; your reprisal (deserved, recompense, reward) shall return upon your own head." Obadiah 15 NIV

While Obadiah was speaking specifically to Edom, his prophecy also has end time application.

Notice also the word 'all.' The 'day of the Lord' will affect all nations.

The day of the Lord according to Zephaniah

The warning to Judah and Jerusalem by the prophet Zephaniah referenced the day of the Lord.

"...for the day of the LORD is near...I will stretch out my hand against Judah and against all who live in Jerusalem... those who turn back from following the LORD...At that time I will search Jerusalem with lamps and punish those who are complacent (indifferent)... Zephaniah 1:4, 7, 12 NIV

Condemnation was directed towards those Israelites who stopped taking God seriously: those who turned their back on God and did it 'their way.'

And impartiality is one of God's attributes, i.e. Israel is treated just like the nations regarding their forgetting God or disobeying His commands and statutes.

Then the worldwide judgment is confirmed.

"The great day of the LORD is near – near and coming quickly...That day will be a day of wrath, a day of distress and anguish, a day of trouble and ruin, a day of darkness and gloom...Neither their silver nor their gold will be able to save them on the day of the LORD's wrath. In the fire of his jealousy the whole world will be consumed..." Zephaniah 1:14-15, 18 NIV

While many nations measure their strength by the size of their economy, such measures will be totally inconsequential in the 'day of the Lord.'

The day of the Lord according to Zechariah

Zechariah describes the great day of the Lord when God would use the nations to chastise Israel.

A day of the LORD is coming when your plunder will be divided among you. I will gather all the nations to Jerusalem to fight against it; the city will be captured... Zechariah 14:1-2 NIV

The day of the Lord according to Malachi

And then approximately 200 years after Zechariah, the final prophet in the Old Testament, i.e. Malachi warns of the approaching day of the Lord.

"Surely the day is coming; it will burn like a furnace. All the arrogant and every evildoer will be stubble, and that day that is coming will set them on fire." Malachi 4:1 NIV

And once again, the 'day' is quickly approaching. The 'day' has been set from the foundation of the world; therefore, each passing day brings God's judgment one day closer to consummation.

The day of the Lord according to John the Baptist and Jesus

At the very beginning of Jesus' ministry, John the Baptist confirmed the coming day of the Lord and warned the Pharisees and Sadducces of such.

But when he (John) saw many of the Pharisees and Sadducees coming to where he was baptizing, he said to them: "You brood of vipers! Who warned you to flee from the coming wrath?" Matthew 3:7 NIV

Four and a half centuries had passed since Malachi, and John and Jesus confirmed the day of the Lord announced earlier by the prophets Isaiah, Jeremiah, Ezekiel, Joel, Amos, Obadiah, Zephaniah, Zechariah, and Malachi.

"Immediately after the distress of those days 'the sun will be darkened, and the moon will not give its light; the stars will fall from the sky, and the heavenly bodies will be shaken.' At that time the sign of the Son of Man will appear in the sky, and all the nations of the earth will mourn. They will see the Son of Man coming on the clouds of the sky, with power and great glory." Matthew 24:29-30 NIV

While the 'world' is in denial and oblivious to such Biblical realities, believers beginning with Jesus' disciples and apostles anticipate His return and the day of the Lord, but the timing has not been revealed.

The day of the Lord according to Paul

'Wrath' in the Greek is very similar to the Hebrew and has several like synonyms including 'indignation,' 'anger,' and 'divine judgment.'

God's wrath will be experienced by all unrepentant mankind.

The wrath of God is being revealed from heaven against all the godlessness and wickedness of men who suppress the truth... Romans 1:18 NIV

"But because of your stubbornness and your unrepentant heart, you are storing up wrath against your self for the day of God's wrath, when his righteous judgment will be revealed. God will give to each person according to what he has done." Romans 2:5 NIV

Those who were treasuring up God's wrath for themselves were unrepentant. Their future judgment will be righteous and will be executed according to one's own deeds. These are the same principles the prophets revealed in the Old Testament.

The great tribulation will be the culmination of God's wrath executed on all mankind up through the age of the church. Men will continue to harden their hearts.

And while God's wrath is poured on all wicked, the Scriptures explicitly state that the redeemed will not experience that wrath. Christ experienced that wrath on our behalf on the cross.

Since we have now been justified by his blood, how much more shall we be saved from God's wrath through him! Romans 5:9 NIV

Paul also taught the Thessalonians that God would send His wrath on those who persecuted them. He also revealed that the Thessalonians would be spared God's wrath on the day of the Lord.

...for they themselves...tell how you turned to God from idols to serve the living and true God, and to wait for his Son from heaven, whom he raised from the dead – Jesus, who rescues us from the coming wrath."
1 Thessalonians 1:9-10 NIV

For God did not appoint us to suffer wrath but to receive salvation through our Lord Jesus Christ. He died for us so that we may live together with him. 1 Thessalonians 5:9-10 NIV

Paul added that the timing of the day of the Lord remained a mystery.

Now, brothers, about times and dates we do not need to write to you, for you know very well that the day of the Lord will come like a thief in the night. While people are saying, "Peace and safety," destruction will come on them suddenly..." 1 Thessalonians 5:1-3 NIV

Saying 'Peace and safety' brings to mind the strategy of the anti-Christ. He will offer a seven year peace treaty between Israel and their enemies. In the midst of the seven year covenant, the anti-Christ will enter the temple and declare himself to be God. No one had suspected such a thing.

In light of all the persecution to be suffered by Christians, Paul admonishes them not to retaliate. Vengeance belongs only to God.

God is just: He will pay back trouble to those who trouble you...This will happen when the Lord Jesus is revealed from heaven in blazing fire with his powerful angels. He will punish those who do not know God and do not obey the gospel of our Lord Jesus. They will be punished with everlasting destruction... 2 Thessalonians 1:6-9 NIV

Do not take revenge, my friends but leave room for God's wrath, for it is written: "It is mine to avenge; I will repay..." Romans 12:19 NIV

The Greek for avenge is very similar to the Hebrew meaning, i.e. to execute justice, or penal retribution.

Likewise 'repay' means to 'requite;' 'to pay in full.'

Israel, God's chosen nation, is oblivious to that which awaits them concerning both the day of the Lord and their redemption and restoration. Their lack of understanding is explained by the following:

"God gave them a spirit of stupor, eyes so that they could not see and ears so that they could not hear, to this very day." Romans 11:8 NIV

Israel will, after the 'day of the Lord,' be the light of the world once again, to fulfill the promises given to Abraham more than 4000 years earlier.

Such a promise has not been given to America.

The day of the Lord according to the writer of Hebrews

The writer of the Book of Hebrews, likewise, invoked the words that God spoke to Moses, when referencing those who despised the significance of Jesus' blood sacrifice in the present age.

How much more severely do you think a man deserves to be punished who has trampled the Son of God under foot, who has treated as an unholy thing the blood of the covenant that sanctified him, and who has insulted the Spirit of grace? For we know him who said, "It is mine to avenge; I will repay..." Hebrews 10:29-30 NIV

Thus, vengeance (penalty, punishment, judgment) will be executed by God Himself. The future imminent judgment is called 'the day of the Lord.'

God's purpose and attributes were revealed in ages past, and have not changed.

Be prepared!

The day of the Lord according to John in the Book of Revelation

The great tribulation will be the culmination of God's wrath executed on all mankind up through the age of the church. The majority of mankind will be unrepentant and continue to harden their hearts.

Then the kings of the earth, the princes, the generals, the rich, the mighty, and every slave and every free man hid in

caves and among the rocks of the mountains. They called to the mountains and the rocks, "Fall on us and hide us from the face of him who sits on the throne and from the wrath of the Lamb! For the great day of their wrath has come, and who can stand?" Revelation 6:15-17 NIV

After the tribulation and millennial kingdom, Satan will be given one last opportunity to deceive those on the earth, but he and his followers will experience God's wrath one last time before the new heaven and earth.

God's vengeance, wrath, recompense, fury, indignation and anger are not very popular doctrines for many churches; however, such are absolute certainties for the disobedient and unrepentant.

Encouragement for the redeemed

O Lord, the God who avenges...shine forth. Rise up, O Judge of the earth; pay back to the proud what they deserve. Psalm 94:1-2 NIV

Similarly Isaiah encourages God's people to maintain their faith; God will not fail to deal with their oppressors.

...say to those with fearful hearts, "Be strong, do not fear; your God will come, he will come with vengeance; with divine retribution he will come to save you." Isaiah 35:4 NIV

God's plan is right on schedule.

Chapter 13

Renewal, Restoration, and Regeneration

It is extremely important to examine significant words in Scripture with their original meaning either from the Hebrew or Greek language. Many times their original meaning does not match the meanings accepted by contemporary English perceptions.

There are two significant Hebrew base words for 'renew.' The first that we'll examine is *chadash* meaning 'renew,' 'repair,' 'rebuild,' or 'fresh.'

The Psalmist spoke of the renewal of the earth.

"You send forth your Spirit (breath)...and You renew the face of the earth." Psalm 104:30 NKJV

Just before God breathed life into Adam...He renewed (rebuilt, repaired) the earth which was without form, and void.

The prophet Jeremiah uses *chadash* several times in his writings.

Restore us to yourself, O LORD, that we may return; renew our days as of old... Lamentations 5:21 NIV

This passage contains three 're' words, i.e. 'restore,' 'return,' and 'renew.' And all three words require God's initiation.

Israel implores God to renew their days, or to return them back again to their previous glory. They are requesting a fresh start.

God addresses the desire of Israel.

"The time is coming," declares the LORD, "when I will make a new covenant with the house of Israel and with the house of Judah. It will not be like the covenant I made with their forefathers..." Jeremiah 31:31-32 NIV

The word 'new' in the above is actually 'renew' from the same Hebrew *chadash*. The renewed covenant will be ratified with the blood of Christ instead of that of animals as in the Mosaic covenant.

New Jerusalem, new heavens and new earth

Recall God's promise of new heavens and new earth.

"Behold, I will create new heavens and a new earth. The former things will not be remembered, nor will they come to mind. But be glad and rejoice forever..." Isaiah 65:17-18 NIV

'Create' in this verse means 'to make,' or 'fashion,' while 'new' in this context means 'to repair,' or 'rebuild.' Likewise New Jerusalem is also from the Hebrew *chadash*.

God will completely redo the present earth; recall 'new' in this verse means 'renew.'

Another significant Hebrew word for 'renew'

A second Hebrew word used for 'renew' in the Old Testament is *chalaph,* meaning 'sprout' or 'change.'

"At least there is hope for a tree: If it is cut down, it will sprout again...Its roots may grow old in the ground...yet at the scent of water it will bud and put forth shoots like a plant..." Job 14:7-9 NIV

The meaning is that even if a tree is cut down, its root system is still alive and will sprout new branches, i.e. will spring up, or be renewed, if watered.

Isaiah uses *chalaph* to describe the strengthening of God's people that trust in Him.

...but those who hope in the LORD will renew their strength. They will soar on wings like eagles; they will run and not grow weary... Isaiah 40:31 NIV

Their strength will be renewed; changed for the better, refreshed from its degraded position.

Several summary thoughts relative to the Hebrew 'renew' are found in the Old Testament.

Renewal can only take place by God's initiation. Renewal always refers to a previous time and situation.

Renewed change is always for the better to improve one's position before Almighty God.

Renewal is our only hope

Not unlike the Hebrew word for 'renewal' in the Old Testament, there are two prominent Greek words interpreted 'renewal' in the New Testament.

The first is *anakainoo* meaning 'to make new again by an act of God.'

The following Scripture passages apply to the renewal of an individual.

Therefore we do not lose heart. Though outwardly we are wasting away, yet inwardly we are being renewed day by day. 2 Corinthians 4:16 NIV

While our physical body is subject to daily decay, the invisible part of the believer is being renewed daily into the image of Christ by an act of God.

You were taught, with regard to your former way of life, to put off your old self, which is being corrupted by its

deceitful desires...and to put on the new self, created to be like God in true righteousness... Ephesians 4:22-24 NIV

Paul was telling the church at Ephesus to abandon the old man which is subject to corruption (decay) and be renewed in the spirit, to return to that which was originally created in God's image.

This teaching was also shared with the church at Colosse.

Do not lie to each other, since you have taken off your old self...and have put on the new self, which is being renewed in knowledge in the image of its Creator. Colossians 3:9-10 NIV

The renewal of a man is initiated by God Himself and each day brings the renewed to the very image of Christ.

New implies better

Renewal is always a change for the better, and man is totally impotent to renew himself.

A similar Greek word for renewal is *kainan* which similarly means a 'change from the old to be renewed to the better.' *Kainan* is the word used to describe the New Covenant. It implies the difference in a man from evil to the Spirit of God; again initiated by God.

Recall the end of the final meal Christ had with His disciples.

Then He took the cup, and gave thanks, and gave it to them, saying, "Drink from it, all of you. For this is My blood of the new covenant, which is shed for many for the remission of sins." Matthew 26:27-28 NKJV

The Greek word for 'new' in this passage is *kainos* (*kainan*) meaning 'renewed,' or 'qualitatively new.' It further means 'different' and 'better than the old.'

The new covenant did not blot out the old; rather it fulfills the original purpose of the old which previously could never be done with the blood of animals. And again, the 'new,' or 'renewed' could only be done if initiated by God.

Remember Paul's great example of the Greek *kainan* in reference to a new believer.

Therefore, if anyone is in Christ, he is a new creation; the old has gone, the new has come! All this is from God... 2 Corinthians 5:17 NIV

Man had the same old corruptible body, but his inner self was renewed.

Paul recounted the words of Jesus when He instituted the Lord's Supper, but he added that drinking of the cup was to remind the disciples of its meaning.

In the same way, after supper he took the cup, saying, "This cup is the new covenant in my blood; do

this, whenever you drink it, in remembrance of me."
1 Corinthians 11:25 NIV

The word 'remembrance' means to 'put in mind again.'
The 're' words that we've studied all have that in common,
i.e. again.

The writer of Hebrews echoed Jeremiah's words, written
700 years prior, relative to the new covenant which would
be instituted by the Lamb of God.

"The time is coming, declares the Lord, when I will
make a new covenant with the house of Israel and with the
house of Judah. It will not be like the covenant I made with
their forefathers..." Hebrews 8:7-9 NIV

The 'new' covenant was a renewal of the 'old.' The
'old' was meant to be temporary until Christ would ratify
the new with His own blood. Also the new covenant could
be honored inasmuch as God would write His laws in the
minds and hearts of His covenant people.

And lastly John saw what Isaiah had spoken of 800
years previous.

Then I saw a new heaven and a new earth, for the first
heaven and the first earth had passed away...
Revelation 21:1 NIV

The physical earth will remain forever; however, it will
be renewed to fulfill the purpose for which it was originally
intended.

Restoration is another significant 're' word

The majority uses of 'restore' in the Old Testament are from the same Hebrew word *shuv* meaning 'repent,' 'return,' and 'again.'

The meaning of 'restore' used in the Scriptures can refer to a number of things ranging from physical property to one's soul.

"Thou shalt not see thy brother's ox or his sheep go astray, and hide thyself from them: thou shalt in any case bring them again unto thy brother...and thou shalt restore it to him..." Deuteronomy 22:1-2 KJV

The law was that if one's animals went astray, his brother (friend, neighbor, relative) shall not ignore them, but rather pursue them and restore them to their rightful owner.

Not only is the word 'restore' from the Hebrew *shuv*, but also the phrase 'bring them again' is from the same Hebrew base. The basic thought is to restore, or return something to its rightful place prior to the subject straying away.

The use of the word 'restore' can also have a short-term application or a long-term application.

For example, when Nebuchadnezzar captured Jerusalem and the temple he did not remove all of the vessels in the temple. Therefore, God instructed that all the remaining vessels be taken to Babylon, but subsequently be returned to the temple in His time. The following is a short term application of 'restore.'

"'They shall be carried to Babylon, and there they shall be until the day that I visit them,' says the LORD. 'Then I will bring them up and restore them to this place.'" Jeremiah 27:22 NKJV

Perhaps the most well-known use of 'restore' is found in Psalms in reference to King David after confessing his sin with Bathsheba and her husband Uriah.

The LORD is my shepherd, I shall not be in want (lack).... he restores my soul. Psalm 23:1, 3 NIV

The subject is the restoration of David's soul upon confession of his sin. The restoration of David's soul could only be done by an act of God. God's restoration is only possible after His gracious forgiveness. David's soul is restored to the point where it was prior to his sin.

In another Psalm David offers a prayer of repentance, and recall, repentance is also from the Hebrew *shuv*.

Create in me a pure heart, O God, and renew a steadfast spirit with me...Restore to me the joy of your salvation... Psalm 51:10, 12 NIV

'Create' in the above has a different meaning than 'to bring to being out of nothing' as we most often think of the word.

In the present context create means 'to do,' or 'to make' (fashion), while 'renew' means 'to repair,' or 'rebuild.'

And restore in Psalm 51:12 above is once again from the Hebrew *shuv* meaning 'to return,' 'back,' or 'again.'

David acknowledges that only God can cleanse his heart and repair his broken spirit. And very significantly, David realizes that the salvation that He pleads to God to restore is not his, but God's.

David's contrition and broken heart are reasons that God called him a man after His own heart.

Thus 'repentance' and 'restore' are very similar and from the same Hebrew base word. Repentance must, however, precede restoration and can only be done by an act of the Holy Spirit.

Likewise, only God can restore a person after He forgives them.

Restoration is the immutable plan of God

As previously stated, the Greek base for 'restore' is very similar to the definitions of 'return.' The basic meaning is 'to put back into a former state.' There are times when the word 'restitution' is used in place of 'restore.'

Recall, the disciples asked Jesus about the timing of the restoration of His kingdom.

"Lord, are you at this time going to restore the kingdom to Israel?" Acts 1:6 NIV

Their question referred to when the lost dominion and authority would be brought back again.

In Peter's second sermon to the crowd at Solomon's temple, he preached on the future restoration of all things at the time of Jesus' return.

"...turn to God...that he may send the Christ, who has been appointed for you – even Jesus. He must remain in heaven until the time comes for God to restore everything, as he promised long ago (since the world began) through his holy prophets." Acts 3:19-21 NIV

Peter's message was that Christ would be in Heaven until the end of Daniel's 70th week, at which time He would return to restore all things. This message was the same preached by the prophets from the beginning. Nothing had changed, nor will God's plan change.

The last Old Testament prophet Malachi announced Christ's first advent and His predecessor, plus His return to earth in the distant future.

He reminded Israel to remember the Law of Moses because their Messiah/King was coming to restore a fallen generation.

Malachi had provided details on Christ's predecessor.

"See, I will send you the prophet Elijah before that great and dreadful day of the LORD comes." Malachi 4:5 NIV

The King would initially arrive on earth following one like Elijah who would announce His coming.

During His first advent, the King would fulfill the Law of Moses and then return to His Father in heaven.

At the exact predetermined time, the King would return to earth to restore it to its original sinless condition.

"And he will restore the hearts of the fathers to their children, and the heart of the children to their fathers..." Malachi 4:6 NASB

For those who refused the sovereignty of the returning King and His restoration, universal judgment would be their fate at 'the great and dreadful day of the LORD.'

'Elijah' was about to arrive

Approximately 420 years after Malachi, the priest Zacharias, the husband of Elizabeth, received a message from an angel of the Lord.

Zacharias was told that he and his wife would bear a son and would call his name John. John would be great in the sight of the Lord and would be filled with the Holy Spirit.

"And he will turn many of the children of Israel to the Lord their God. He will also go before Him in the spirit and power of Elijah, 'to turn the hearts of the fathers to the children...'" Luke 1:16-17a NKJV

'Turn' in this verse means 'to return,' i.e. 'come back again.' The most common synonym would be 'repent.'

Recall the transfiguration scene when Peter, James, and John were in the presence of the glorified Jesus who appeared to be talking with Moses and Elijah. At that time the disciples asked Jesus why the scribes say that Elijah must come before Jesus.

Jesus replied, "To be sure, Elijah comes and will restore all things. But I tell you, Elijah has already come, and they did not recognize him, but have done to him everything they wished." Matthew 17:11-12 NIV

'Restore' in this verse again means 'to bring back a lost dominion,' or 'restitution of something to its former condition.'

Jesus subsequently identified 'Elijah' as John the Baptist.

Then the disciples understood that he was talking about John the Baptist. Matthew 17:13 NIV

The basic message of John was to 'repent.' The word 'repent' in the present context means 'a turning from unbelief and sin to God;' 'to come back again,' 'to return.'

Jesus said that John the Baptist had come to restore 'all things.'

Recall, 'restore' similarly means to 'put back into former state; return.'

Regeneration is another Biblical 're' word

One other similar word to mention is 'regeneration' from the Greek *paliggenesia* meaning 'again,' 'renew,' and 'restore.' It can apply to individuals as well to all things.

"So Jesus said to them, 'Assuredly I say to you, that in the regeneration, when the Son of Man sits on the throne of His glory, you who have followed Me will also sit on twelve thrones...'" Matthew 19:28 NKJV

Paul writes of the regenerative works of God on His people.

"...but according to His mercy He saved us, through the washing of regeneration and renewing of the Holy Spirit, whom He poured out on us abundantly through Jesus Christ..." Titus 3:5-6 NKJV

'Regeneration' in this verse means 'spiritual rebirth of the individual soul.' Another appropriate synonym is 'rebirth.'

The major point in this chapter is that God's entire plan will be fulfilled through Christ, which is to bring all things back to the time and place before sin entered the world.

Solomon had it right along

What has been will be again, what has been done will be done again; there is nothing new under the sun.
Ecclesiastes 1:9 NIV

Chapter 14

In that Day

We've learned that the phrase 'the day of the Lord' is very significant in the Bible. The day of the Lord predominantly has reference to the seven year tribulation period and/or the time of Christ's return to end the tribulation.

'In that day' for the most part refers to the millennium commencing immediately following Christ's triumphant return to end 'the day of the Lord.' Another common phrase used in the Bible to express the future kingdom is 'latter days.'

Thus, while the day of the Lord speaks of God's vengeance and wrath, 'in that day' speaks of His redemption and restoration, primarily of His chosen nation Israel. 'In that day' describes the earthly kingdom preceding the 'new heaven and new earth.'

To describe the kingdom following the tribulation, we'll address four major issues.

- The location of the kingdom

- The ruler of the kingdom

- Characteristics of the kingdom

- Past enemies of the kingdom

Of a surety, a lengthy book could be written on each of the four major issues; however, we'll attempt to identify and list several significant points of each to give a brief understanding of each issue.

- **The location of the kingdom**

The future kingdom will be in the same area as the original land promised to Abraham four thousand years earlier. God's covenant with Abraham, which included the borders of the Promised Land, was immutable and eternal.

On that day the LORD made a covenant with Abram and said, "To your descendants I give this land, from the river of Egypt to the great river, the Euphrates..."
Genesis 15:18 NIV

"The whole land of Canaan, where you are now an alien, I will give as an everlasting possession to you and your descendants after you; and I will be their God."
Genesis 17:8 NIV

The above two verses define the extent of the promised land, the duration of the promise, the inheritance of Abraham's descendants, and the promise that God would be the God of Abraham and his descendants forever.

The extent of the Promised Land will displace several nations that presently occupy portions of the land.

A nation can also be identified by its capital

God told Moses in advance that He would choose His permanent dwelling place within the land.

But you are to seek the place the LORD your God will choose from among all your tribes to put his Name there for his dwelling. To that place you must go...
Deuteronomy 12:5 NIV

Approximately five centuries later, when Abraham's descendant David assumed kingship over all Israel, God directed him to the city of the Jebusites called Jerusalem.

The king (David) and his men marched to Jerusalem to attack the Jebusites, who lived there. The Jebusites said to David, "you will not get in here..." Nevertheless, David captured the fortress of Zion, the City of David.
2 Samuel 5:6-7 NIV

Jerusalem was henceforth called the 'City of David.'

David was not allowed to build a temple for God at Jerusalem; however, God had instructed David that his son Solomon would build Him a temple there.

Then Solomon began to build the temple of the LORD in Jerusalem on Mount Moriah, where the LORD had appeared to his father David...He began building on the second day of the second month in the fourth year of his reign. 2 Chronicles 3:1-2 NIV

At the dedication of the completed temple, Solomon recounted God's words to his father David.

"Since the day I brought my people out of Egypt, I have not chosen a city in any tribe of Israel to have a temple built for my Name to be there, nor have I chosen anyone to be the leader over my people Israel. But now I have chosen Jerusalem for my Name to be there, and I have chosen David to rule my people Israel." 2 Chronicles 6:5-8 NIV

Jeremiah recorded the word of the LORD regarding His dwelling place 'in that day.'

At that time (in that day) they will call Jerusalem The Throne of the LORD, and all nations will gather in Jerusalem to honor the name of the LORD. Jeremiah 3:17 NIV

And Ezekiel recorded God's words spoken from the temple to be built in Jerusalem 'in that day.'

"...Son of man, this is the place of my throne and the place for the soles of my feet. This is where I will live among the Israelites forever." Ezekiel 43:7 NIV

Therefore, the future earthly kingdom 'in that day' will be located in the land originally granted to Abraham for an everlasting possession, and the capital city of the kingdom will be Jerusalem. In fact, Ezekiel foretells that God will dwell with His people in the age following the millennial kingdom, i.e. the age of 'New Jerusalem.'

- **The ruler of the kingdom**

The family tree of the ruler of the future kingdom was identified shortly after the location of the kingdom was revealed. It began with Abraham, then his son Isaac, and then Isaac's son Jacob.

Shortly before Jacob died in Egypt, he called his sons together.

"And Jacob called his sons and said, 'Gather together, that I may tell you what shall befall you in the last days.'" Genesis 49:1 NKJV

Then he proceeded to reveal the future of each of his sons. Of particular interest were his words concerning his son Judah.

"Judah, your brothers will praise you...The scepter will not depart from Judah, nor the ruler's staff from between his feet, until he comes to whom it belongs and the obedience of the nations is his." Genesis 49:8, 10 NIV

Even though Judah was not the oldest of Jacob's sons, his future was the most significant. Judah's brothers would bow down to him in the future. In addition Judah would provide the 'seed' not only for the future king of Israel, but for all people on earth.

Therefore, the future king would come through Abraham, Isaac, Jacob, and Judah...

Approximately eight centuries later, the future king from the family of Judah was defined in more detail.

God provided details of His covenant with Abraham

God spoke to King David through the prophet Nathan.

"When your days are over and you rest with your fathers, I will raise up your offspring to succeed you, who will come from your own body, and I will establish his kingdom...and I will establish the throne of his kingdom forever." 2 Samuel 7:12-13 NIV

Of course David's son Solomon would immediately succeed him, but David's later descendants through Solomon, and Solomon's brother Nathan, would provide the ultimate king for the kingdom 'in that day.'

Isaiah was one of the prophets chosen to announce the future king.

For to us a child is born, to us a son is given, and the government will be on his shoulder...He will reign on David's throne and over his kingdom...from that time on and forever. Isaiah 9:6-7 NIV

Isaiah confirmed the words spoken to David centuries prior. Isaiah announced that the future king would be the head of government, and that his kingdom would never end.

Isaiah reveals details of the earthly lineage of the future king.

A shoot will come up from the stump of Jesse; from his roots a Branch will bear fruit. The Spirit of the LORD will rest on him – the Spirit of wisdom and of understanding, the Spirit of counsel and of power, the Spirit of knowledge and of the fear of the LORD. Isaiah 11:1-2 NIV

The future king would be from the family of Jesse and would possess ultimate wisdom and understanding. He would be under the direct sovereignty of Almighty God Himself.

Jesse was the earthly father of David.

Subsequently, God provided more details to the prophet Jeremiah.

"'Behold, the days are coming,' says the LORD, 'that I will perform that good thing which I have promised to the house of Israel and to the house of Judah: In those days and at that time I will cause to grow up to David a Branch of righteousness; He shall execute judgment and righteousness in the earth...' For thus says the LORD: 'David shall never lack a man to sit on the throne of the house of Israel.'" Jeremiah 33:14-15, 17 NKJV

Hosea confirmed that in the future Israel's king, the Branch of David, would reign over the repentant of Israel.

"Afterward the children of Israel shall return and seek the LORD their God and David their king. They shall fear the LORD and His goodness in the latter days."
Hosea 3:5 NKJV

Inasmuch as the nation of Israel will once again be the light of the millennial kingdom; much is said relative to God's chosen 'in that day.'

In that day the remnant of Israel...will return to the Mighty God. Though your people, O Israel, be like the sand of the sea, only a remnant will return. Isaiah 10:20-22 NIV

Even though Israel was/is and will be God's chosen nation forever, only a remnant will be saved. Israel 'in that day' will return to their God and never again be subject to foreign domination.

"In the whole land," declares the LORD, "two-thirds will be struck down and perish; yet one-third will be left in it. This third I will bring into the fire; I will refine them like silver and test them like gold. They will call on my name and I will answer them; I will say, 'They are my people,' and they will say, 'The LORD is our God.'"
Zechariah 13:8-9 NIV

Prophecy becomes reality

Now let's fast forward five centuries after Zechariah to the beginning of the Gospels.

The context is the message Gabriel brought to the young woman named Mary.

But the angel said to her, "Do not be afraid, Mary, you have found favor with God. You will be with child and give birth to a son, and you are to give him the name Jesus. He will be great and will be called the Son of the Most High. The LORD God will give him the throne of his father David, and he will reign over the house of Jacob forever; his kingdom will never end." Luke 1:30-31 NIV

All of the quoted prophecies are being fulfilled in Jesus. He is the Son of God, the offspring of David, and He will rule over the house of Jacob forever.

The genealogy of Jesus confirms His family tree.

"The book of the genealogy of Jesus Christ, the Son of David, the Son of Abraham: Abraham begot Isaac, Isaac begot Jacob, and Jacob begot Judah. Judah begot Perez, and Perez...begot Boaz, Boaz begot Obed, Obed begot Jesse, and Jesse begot David the king." Matthew 1:1-3, 5-6 NKJV

And inasmuch as we began this section in Genesis, it is only fitting that we end this section with Jesus' own words from the final Book of the Bible.

"I, Jesus, have sent my angel to give you this testimony for the churches. I am the Root and the Offspring of David, and the bright Morning Star." Revelation 22:16 NIV

As deity, Jesus was from the foundation of the world; hence He is the ancestor, or root, of David. As the Seed of the woman, He is also the offspring of David. He is both.

• **Characteristics of the kingdom**

The kingdom 'in that day' will be totally different than the kingdoms and nations as we know them today. The future kingdom will be the precursor of the New Jerusalem, and the new heavens and earth.

All those returning with Christ after the tribulation, and those who survived the tribulation, will honor the king in the capital city of Jerusalem.

"Now it shall come to pass in the latter days that the mountain of the LORD's house shall be established on the top of the mountains...and peoples shall flow to it." Micah 4:1 NKJV

Judgment has been completed, and only God's people will populate the earth and the millennial kingdom, to begin with.

All saved nations will hunger for the word and wisdom of the king.

Many nations will come and say, "Come, let us go up to the mountain of the LORD, to the house of the God of Jacob, He will teach us his ways, so that we may walk in his paths." The law will go out from Zion...He will judge between many peoples and will settle disputes for strong nations far and wide. Micah 4:2-3a NIV

Wars will have ended before the time of the millennial kingdom. The nations will be instructed to relinquish their weapons in favor of useful tools to be used in the kingdom.

They will beat their swords into plowshares and their spears into pruning hooks. Nation will not take up sword against nation, nor will they train for war anymore. Micah 4:3b NIV

There will be peace and prosperity for all citizens of the kingdom. Everyone will display acts of kindness and sharing to his neighbor.

Whereas Israel was formerly a vineyard which did not produce acceptable fruit, all will be changed 'in that day.'

"'In that day' sing to her, 'A vineyard of red wine! I, the LORD, keep it, I water it every moment; lest any hurt it, I keep it night and day...Those who come He shall cause to take root in Jacob; Israel shall blossom and bud, and fill the face of the world with fruit...And it shall come to pass in that day that the LORD will thresh, from the channel of the River (Euphrates) to the Brook of Egypt; and you will be gathered one by one, O you children of Israel. So it shall

be in that day: The great trumpet will be blown; they will come...and shall worship the LORD in the holy mount at Jerusalem.'" Isaiah 27:2-3, 6, 12-13 NKJV

Again, Israel will be the center piece of the millennial kingdom. God will gather His people from the four 'winds' to their own land, defined as the Brook of Egypt to the Euphrates River, and refine them. Recall, such is the defined boundaries of the land promised to them back in the early chapters of Genesis.

"In that day each of you will invite his neighbor to sit under his vine and fig tree," declares the LORD Almighty. Zechariah 3:10 NIV

And then Hosea speaks of the abundant production in the land 'in that day.'

"In that day I will respond," declares the LORD – "I will respond to the skies, and they will respond to the earth; and the earth will respond to the grain, the new wine and oil, and they will respond to Jezreel (God will sow). I will plant her for myself in the land; I will show my love to the one I called 'Not my loved one.' I will say to those called 'Not my people, You are my people'; and they will say 'You are my God.'" Hosea 2:21-23 NIV

'In that day' the needs of the earth to produce in abundance will flow upwards to the heavens (sky), and God will hear (answer) to the needs and respond downward to the earth to provide grain, new wine, and oil in abundance.

Prayer will be a top priority among all citizens of the kingdom. There is one 'religion' and one God, i.e. the God of Israel and Jerusalem.

"...and the inhabitants of one city will go to another and say, 'Let us go at once to entreat the LORD and seek the LORD Almighty... And many peoples and powerful nations will come to Jerusalem to seek the LORD Almighty and to entreat him." Zechariah 8:21-22 NIV

Citizens from all nations in the kingdom will cling to the Jew and desire to know their God.

This is what the LORD Almighty says: "In those days ten men from all languages and nations will take firm hold of one Jew by the hem of his robe and say, 'Let us go with you, because we have heard that God is with you."' Zechariah 8:23 NIV

The true, eternal light

In reality, the presence of God is the light for the kingdom.

"Arise, shine, for your light has come, and the glory of the LORD rises upon you." Isaiah 60:1 NIV

'Light' in this verse is from the Hebrew *owr* meaning, 'enlightenment,' or 'glory.'

It is the same word found in the following well known Scripture passages.

And God said, "Let there be light," and there was light. Genesis 1:3 NIV

...God...says: "It is too small a thing for you to be my servant to restore the tribes of Jacob and bring back those of Israel I have kept. I will also make you a light for the Gentiles, that you may bring my salvation to the ends of the earth." Isaiah 49:6 NIV

Such 'light' is the very presence of God as was evidenced by the Shekinah Glory in days of old.

Government in the kingdom

In America there are three distinct branches of government, i.e. the executive branch, the legislative branch (the house and senate), and the judicial branch (federal courts and Supreme Court.)

All three functions will also be present in the millennial kingdom; however, the king Himself will fulfill all three functions.

For the LORD is our judge, the LORD is our lawgiver, the LORD is our king; it is he who will save us. Isaiah 33:22 NIV

America is considered to be a constitutional republic which is defined as a state where the officials are elected as representatives of the people and must govern according to an existing constitution.

In a pure democracy the majority of citizens have nearly direct rule with fewer restrictions than found in a republic where the people's voice is expressed through elected representatives.

In stark contrast, the government of the millennial kingdom will be a monarchy where there is undivided rule or absolute sovereignty by a single person; a government having one hereditary chief of state with life tenure.

The psalmist describes the government and ruler of the future kingdom. The LORD God says:

"I have installed my King on Zion, my holy hill."
Psalm 2:8 NIV

The King replies:

I will proclaim the decree of the LORD: He said to me, "You are my Son; today I have become your Father. Ask of me, and I will make the nations your inheritance, the ends of the earth your possession. You will rule them with an iron scepter; you will dash them to pieces like pottery."
Psalm 2:7-9 NIV

The above passage fits the definition of a textbook monarchy.

There will be no appeals, there will be no need for senate or house majority votes, and there will be no need for the chief executive to sign proposed legislation. There will be no special prosecutors or grand jury investigations.

Israel was predestined to produce the King, and it was also predestined that He would rule with a rod of iron.

She gave birth to a son, a male child, who will rule all the nations with an iron scepter. And her child was snatched up to God and to his throne. Revelation 12:5 NIV

That authority was confirmed later in the Book of Revelation where John saw the return of the King.

"Now I saw heaven opened, and behold, a white horse. And He who sat on him was called Faithful and True, and in righteousness He judges and makes war...Now out of His mouth goes a sharp sword, that with it He should strike the nations. And He Himself will rule them with a rod of iron..." Revelation 19:11, 15 NKJV

The Greek meaning of 'rod' means 'scepter.'

To rule them 'with a rod of iron' takes us back to Jacob's proclamation cited earlier in this chapter concerning the future of his son Judah.

The scepter will not depart from Judah, nor the ruler's (lawgiver's) staff from between his feet, until he comes to

whom it belongs and the obedience of the nations is his.
Genesis 49:10 NIV

The word 'scepter' in the Hebrew likewise means 'rod,' while 'lawgiver' has several relative synonyms including 'decree' and 'rule.'

Shared rule

Those who prevailed from the church at Thyatira were also promised the power to rule nations with a rod of iron.

"To him who overcomes and does my will to the end, I will give authority over the nations – He will rule them with an iron scepter; he will dash them to pieces like pottery – just as I have received authority from my Father."
Revelation 2:26-27 NIV

That's not all; recall, Paul revealed that much power would be given to saints.

Do you not know that the saints will judge the world? And if you are to judge the world...Do you not know that we will judge angels? 1 Corinthians 6:2-3 NIV

The Greek word for 'judge' in the present context means 'to discern' or 'to discriminate' between good and evil upon examining the law.

- **Past enemies of the kingdom**

The ancestors of the ruler of the future kingdom had many enemies. In fact, national Israel had many more enemies than friends.

The majority of mankind will not participate in the kingdom.

However, it must be kept in mind that there will be a remnant from every nation, tribe, and people group on earth.

Remnants from all nations, even those nations that hated Israel, will worship the King in Jerusalem.

Then the survivors from all the nations that have attacked Jerusalem will go up year after year to worship the King, the LORD Almighty... Zechariah 14:26 NIV

The sons of your oppressors will come bowing before you; all who despise you will bow down at your feet and will call you the City of the LORD, Zion of the Holy One of Israel. Isaiah 60:14 NIV

The kings of Tarshish and of distant shores will bring tribute to him; the kings of Sheba and Seba will present him gifts. All kings will bow down to him and all nations will serve him. Psalm 72:10-11 NIV

In fact, the ships of Tarshish will bring dispersed Jews back to Israel along with their silver and gold.

This is what the LORD says: "The products of Egypt and their merchandise of Cush, and those tall Sabeans – they will come over to you and will be yours...They will bow down before you and plead with you, saying, 'Surely God is with you, and there is no other; there is no other god.'" Isaiah 45:14 NIV

Least likely servants

Offspring of Ishmael and the sons of Abraham by Keturah who had journeyed to the east and Arabia will honor the King.

...the wealth of the seas will be brought to you, to you the riches of the nations will come. Herds of camels will cover your land, young camels of Midian and Ephah, and all from Sheba will come, bearing gold and incense and proclaiming the praise of the LORD. Isaiah 60:5-6 NIV

There will even be a remnant from the nations that God had previously used to chastise Israel for their past sins.

But there is a stern warning. If anyone from any nation who survived the tribulation does not serve the king, they shall be cut off.

For the nation or kingdom that will not serve you will perish; it will be utterly ruined. Isaiah 60:12 NIV

And the Bible has several surprises relative to Israel's past enemies.

In that day there will be a highway from Egypt to Assyria. The Assyrians will go to Egypt and Egyptians to Assyria. The Egyptians and Assyrians will worship together. In that day Israel will be the third, along with Egypt and Assyria, a blessing on the earth. The LORD Almighty will bless them, saying, "Blessed be Egypt my people, Assyria my handiwork, and Israel my inheritance. Isaiah 19:23-25 NIV

Try telling that to the United Nations today.

Chapter 15

Remember

'Remember' is a fitting word to finish our journey.

In Old Testament Hebrew, 'remember' has several common synonyms including 'recollect,' 'recount,' or 'to bring up a memory again.'

In the Old Testament the Israelites were told time and time again to remember the historical sovereign acts of God which He did on their behalf. In reality, Israel's success or failures were based on what they had remembered, or forgotten.

In New Testament Greek, 'remember' is said to be a God-given gift to keep certain thoughts and memories fresh in one's mind for learning and interpretation of future events and circumstances. 'Remember' means 'to bring to mind or deliberate.'

The Greek word primarily used for 'remember' is *mnaomai,* meaning 'to exercise one's memory.'

In the New Testament the word 'remember' is used predominately to bring to mind what Jesus had taught.

Webster's contemporary meaning is basically the same as the Hebrew and Greek, i.e. to consciously exercise one's memory to bring to mind some past event or words.

Thus 'remember' corresponds with other 're' words previously covered with the basic meaning to 'go back again.'

Israel was told to remember their plight and God's deliverance

One of the earliest and most significant applications of 'remember' is found nearly immediately after Israel was redeemed out of bondage from Egypt.

"And Moses said to the people: 'Remember this day in which you went out of Egypt, out of the house of bondage; for by strength of hand the LORD brought you out of this place...'" Exodus 13:3 NKJV

Israel was told numerous times throughout the Old Testament to remember their previous time of slavery and bondage in the hands of the Egyptians.

Following the giving of the law, Moses told the Israelites to remember all of God's commandments. They were told to place tassels on their garments as reminders.

Then the LORD said to Moses... "you are to make tassels on the corners of your garments...You will have these tassels to look at and so you will remember all the commands of the LORD, that you may obey them..." Numbers 15:37-39 NIV

And then just prior to crossing the Jordon, the Israelites were told to remember how their God had provided for them during the wilderness journey.

Remember how the LORD your God led you all the way in the desert these forty years, to humble you and to test you in order to know what was in your heart, whether or not you would keep his commands. Deuteronomy 8:2 NIV

Before possessing the land, Moses wrote a 'song' describing Israel's future history. The purpose of the song was to tell Israel in advance what they would do and think. The song was to be a testimony to them when the words of the song became reality.

"Remember the days of old, consider the years of many generations. Ask your father, and he will show you...When the Most High divided their inheritance to the nations, when He separated the sons of Adam, He set the boundaries of the peoples according to the number of the children of Israel..." Deuteronomy 32:7-8 NKJV

Approximately 400 years later when David assumed the kingship of Israel, he placed the Ark of the Covenant in a tabernacle that he had erected for it in Jerusalem. On that day he offered the following psalm to thank his LORD God.

Remember the wonders he has done, his miracles, and the judgments he pronounced, O descendants of Israel his servant, O sons of Jacob, his chosen ones.
1 Chronicles 16:12-13 NIV

David wrote numerous psalms extolling the sovereignty of His God. He wrote the following depicting the correct preparedness for battle.

"Some trust in chariots, and some in horses; but we will remember the name of the LORD our God."
Psalm 20:7 NKJV

All the military strength of a nation cannot compare to placing trust in God.

And then David describes the everlasting mercy of God bestowed on those who remember Him, compared to the transitory nature of mortal man.

"As for man, his days are like grass; as a flower of the field...For the wind passes over it, and it is gone, and its place remembers it no more. But the mercy of the LORD is from everlasting to everlasting on those who fear Him...and to those who remember His commandments to do them."
Psalm 103:15-18 NKJV

Remember is not quite the same as 'not to forget'

While remember means to consciously exercise one's God given gift to bring something to mind from the past, 'forget' means to be oblivious to something due to lack of attention. Therefore, the Bible lists many significant words or events that God's people were told 'not to forget.'

In many cases the Israelites were told not to forget things they had been previously told to remember.

When God reminded Israel that they were His chosen nation He stressed that they were to remain diligent; especially regarding keeping His law.

"Only take heed to yourself, and diligently keep yourself, lest you forget the things your eyes have seen...and teach them to your children and your grandchildren, especially concerning the day you stood before the LORD your God in Horeb..." Deuteronomy 4:9 NKJV

God subsequently warned the Israelites that when His blessings began to fall upon them in the Promised Land, such as living in houses and cities they did not build, wells they did not dig, etc., they must not forget their Provider.

"...lest – when you have eaten and are full, and have built beautiful houses and dwell in them...when your heart is lifted up, and you forget the LORD your God who brought you out of the land of Egypt, from the house of bondage..." Deuteronomy 8:12 NKJV

In the final chapters of Deuteronomy, Moses recounted God's grace on Israel. Moses then revealed the curse that would ensnare Israel if they were prideful.

The curse would be so devastating that the surrounding nations would inquire as to why the LORD had done this to His own people.

"Then people would say: 'Because they have forsaken the covenant of the LORD God of their fathers, which He made with them when He brought them out of the land of Egypt; for they went and served other gods...'"
Deuteronomy 29:25-26 NKJV

'Forsaken' is even more disastrous than 'forget.' It means 'to consciously leave or abandon.'

Israel did exactly what God had said not to do

After the death of Joshua, the people further forsook the LORD God.

Then the Israelites did evil in the eyes of the LORD and served the Baals. They forsook the LORD, the God of their fathers, who had brought them out of Egypt.
Judges 2:11-12 NIV

The Psalmist Asaph admonished rebellious Israel to turn back to God.

"For He established a testimony in Jacob, and appointed a law in Israel...that the generation to come might know them...that they may set their hope in God, and not forget the works of God..." Psalm 78:5-7 NKJV

The Israelites were not only to remember God's laws, but also to teach them to future generations so that their children and grandchildren would know God and His wondrous works, and not forget them.

David echoed the words of Asaph.

"Bless the LORD, O my soul, and forget not all His benefits (gifts, reward)." Psalm 103:2 NIV

David's son Solomon accepted God's laws as his own and taught his sons accordingly.

My son, do not forget my teaching, but keep my commands in your heart, for they will prolong your life many years and bring you prosperity. Proverbs 3:1 NIV

False prophets were a snare to Israel

Jeremiah reported that false prophets attempted to cause the Israelites to forget that they were God's people.

"...Indeed they are prophets of the deceit of their own heart, who try to make My people forget My name..." Jeremiah 23:26-27 NKJV

False prophets will pay the price.

"...therefore behold, I...will utterly forget you and forsake you...and I will bring an everlasting reproach upon you, and a perpetual shame, which shall not be forgotten." Jeremiah 23:39-40 NKJV

God will never forget or forsake the remnant of Israel

The prophet Isaiah spoke of the time when Jerusalem thought that their God had abandoned them.

"But Zion said, 'The LORD has forsaken me, and my Lord has forgotten me.' 'Can a woman forget her nursing child...surely they may forget, yet I will not forget you.'" Isaiah 49:14-15 NKJV

God said that it would be easier for a nursing mother to forget her child, than for Him to forget His people, Israel.

However, Israel forgot and forsook their God and would suffer tremendous consequences; however, due to God's covenant with Abraham, the remnant would be redeemed and restored.

America has no such promise; what will her future be?

Remembering the words of Jesus

Recall, the primary meaning of 'remembering' from the Greek is to exercise one's God given gift of bringing to mind words and events from previous teachings. Such remembrance enhances learning and provides a means to interpret future events and circumstances.

Thus far in our study of remembrance, all Scriptural references were limited to the Old Testament. Now we'll look at several New Testament passages from the gospels, epistles, and the final book in the Bible.

The disciple John quoted Jesus when He revealed a major blessing of the future Comforter.

"But the Helper, the Holy Spirit, whom the Father will send in My name, He will teach you all things, and bring to your remembrance all things that I said to you."
John 14:26 NKJV

The God-given gift of remembrance will be accomplished through the Holy Spirit during the age of the church.

Not only would the Holy Spirit teach Christ's followers all things, He would bring to their minds all things that Jesus had spoken to them.

One of the many things that Jesus taught His disciples to remember was that the world would hate them as the world hated Him.

"As it is, you do not belong to the world, but I have chosen you out of the world. That is why the world hates you. Remember the words I spoke to you: 'No servant is greater than his master.' If they persecuted me, they will persecute you also." John 15:19-20 NIV

Perhaps the greatest teaching of Jesus to His disciples related to the New Covenant that He introduced during His final supper with them.

And he took bread, gave thanks and broke it, and gave it to them, saying, "This is my body given for you; do this in remembrance of me." Luke 22:19 NIV

Jesus was the Bread of Life!

Remembering can also cause tremendous humility and grief. Recall Peter proclaimed that he would never deny Christ; however, Jesus told Peter that Peter would deny Him three times during the hours before His appearance before Pilate.

Upon the third accusation that Peter was with Christ in the garden, the words foretold by Jesus were fulfilled.

Immediately a rooster crowed. Then Peter remembered the word Jesus has spoken: "Before the rooster crows, you will disown (deny) me three times." And he went outside and wept bitterly. Matthew 26:74-75 NIV

Then after Christ's resurrection, the first women who came to His tomb were perplexed that the tomb was empty. Two angels standing nearby explained the phenomena.

"...Why do you seek the living among the dead? He is not here, but is risen! Remember how He spoke to you when He was still in Galilee, saying, 'The Son of Man must be delivered into the hands of sinful men, and be crucified, and the third day rise again.' And they remembered His words..." Luke 24:5-8 NKJV

After Christ's ascension, Paul taught the words of Jesus when He introduced the New Covenant to the church at Corinth.

For I received from the LORD what I also passed on to you: The Lord Jesus, on the night he was betrayed, took bread...In the same way, after supper he took the cup, saying, "This cup is the new covenant in my blood; do this, whenever you drink it, in remembrance of me."
1 Corinthians 11:23, 25 NIV

Subsequently while Paul was telling those at Ephesus of his imminent departure, he said:

In everything I did, I showed you...we must help the weak, remembering the words the Lord Jesus himself said: "It is more blessed to give than to receive." Acts 20:35 NIV

Paul admonished the church leaders at Ephesus to remember the words of Jesus.

And in the final book in the Bible, Jesus spoke to John about the seven churches beginning with the church at Ephesus. He first commended them for their recognition of hypocrites, and their patience and labor.

"Yet I hold this against you: You have forsaken your first love. Remember the height from which you have fallen! Repent and do the things you did at first..."
Revelation 2:4-5 NIV

Two highly significant 're' words are found in this passage, i.e. 'remember' and 'repent.'

Not all things will be remembered

There are certain things that God's people plead to Him not to remember. And just as it is a gift of God to be able to remember, it is a gift of God for Him to not remember certain things in the life of a nation or individual.

David explains such phenomena.

"Remember, O LORD, Your tender mercies and Your lovingkindnesses, for they are from of old. Do not remember the sins of my youth nor my transgressions; according to Your mercy remember me, for Your goodness' sake, O LORD." Psalm 25:6-7 NKJV

Initially David asks God to remember His attribute of mercy by not remembering David's sins from his younger days. Then David pleads for God to remember him as His child created in God's own image.

David remembered that all sins have deadly consequences and he could only be justified by God's mercy.

The psalmist Asaph uttered a similar plea.

"Oh (LORD), do not remember former iniquities against us! Let Your tender mercies come speedily to meet us, for we have been brought very low (oppressed)." Psalm 79:8 NKJV

Asaph also acknowledged that only God had the power and authority not to remember sins.

The prophet Isaiah confirmed that God could and would forgive and forget sins of His people for His own sake upon the sinner's repentance.

"I, even I, am he who blots out your transgressions, for my own sake, and remembers your sins no more." Isaiah 43:25 NIV

God's forgiveness for His own sake relates to His immutable covenant with Abraham.

Approximately a century after Isaiah, Jeremiah also addressed the sins of Israel as a nation.

Israel's sins must be forgiven and forgotten, inasmuch as Israel would be major benefactors of the New Covenant.

"But this is the covenant that I will make with the house of Israel after those days, says the LORD...No more shall every man teach his neighbor, and every man his brother, saying, 'know the LORD,' for they all shall know Me, from the least of them to the greatest of them...For I will forgive their iniquity, and their sin I will remember no more." Jeremiah 31:33-34 NKJV

Notice the 'I will' phrases in this passage. '...the covenant that I will make,' 'I will forgive their iniquity,' and 'their sin I will remember no more.'

Summary statement

Some of the grandest aspects of the new heavens and new earth include things that will not be.

"And God will wipe away every tear from their eyes; there shall be no more death, nor sorrow, nor crying. There shall be no more pain, for the former things have passed away." Revelation 21:4 NKJV

Recall approximately 800 years before John wrote the above, Isaiah spoke of the new heavens and new earth, but added a major detail.

"...And the former shall not be remembered or come to mind." Isaiah 65:17b NKJV

Therefore, not only will the curse and its affects be gone, there will be no remembrance of such former things.

Thus while the world, including America, is intrigued with such ideology as progressivism, God's plan is better defined as reversion, i.e. returning to a former state or condition.

The keys to understanding God's plan, therefore, include such words as return, repent, redeem, renew, and restore.

The sovereignty of Almighty God is unfathomable to the finite mind. His plan for those created in His own image was devised before the foundation of the world.

In order to implement His immutable plan, He must initiate the actions of man at the exact pre-determined time.

Thus, while God's sovereignty reigns supreme, the naiveté and impotency of man is humbly revealed.

About the Author

From Prophecy to Reality is the fourth book the author has written in this genre. His previous books include 1) America's Vision vs. God's Standard of Justice 2) God's Plan for His Chosen, and 3) Looking Backward from the Future.

Upon receiving his education at California State University, he served two decades with several blue chip firms in the industrial sector. He then entered academia and served 15 years as assistant professor at Northeastern

Oklahoma State University in the College of Business and Technology.

He has been published in such trade journals as Journal of Industrial Engineering, Management Accounting, and Pecan South. He has also written more than 500 newspaper columns on Biblical issues.

He is a veteran of the USMC and is a voluntary Chaplin at a veterans center.

Printed in the United States
By Bookmasters